NORMS&
NOBILITY

NORMS&
NOBILITY
A TREATISE ON EDUCATION

DAVID V. HICKS

PRAEGER SPECIAL STUDIES • PRAEGER SCIENTIFIC

Published in 1981 by Praeger Publishers
CBS Educational and Professional Publishing
A Division of CBS, Inc.
521 Fifth Avenue, New York, New York 10175 U.S.A.

© 1981 by Praeger Publishers

Library of Congress Catalog Card Number: 81-2447

0-03-059273-9

123456789   145   987654321

Printed in the United States of America

ACKNOWLEDGMENTS

Unless otherwise noted, the observations and interpretations recorded in this book are my own; however, they were not arrived at in isolation. I owe a great debt of thanks to those who, whether affirming or opposing my argument, helped me to make it. I thank Donn Gaebelein, president of the Westminster Schools in Atlanta, for providing me with the opportunity to study the problems of curricular reform first-hand. For graciously tolerating my intrusions, I thank the Westminster faculty, especially Tom McIntyre, whose Attic wit and wisdom guided my early steps.

While developing my ideas I visited several outstanding schools, and I want to acknowledge with gratitude the honest, intelligent, and sometimes provocative responses I received to my queries at each of these: Phillips Exeter, Portsmouth Abbey, St. George's School, Choate-Rosemary Hall, the Stony Brook School, and the Horace Mann School. I want also to thank the board of trustees and my faculty colleagues at St. Andrew's for their imaginative and tireless efforts to put into practice much of the curriculum proposal contained in this book.

Professor John Crossett of Cornell College honored me with a rigorous criticism of Chapter 1; if my abilities as a writer were equal to his skills as a teacher, these words would conjure up new worlds. I thank George Zimmar, my editor and friend, for his unfailing encouragement; Carl Walter and Paul Kane, for their critical readings of the manuscript; and Louise Gray, for her careful clerical assistance.

Most of all, I value the forbearing love of my wife, who, while still a bride, shared the writer with his book, which we dedicate to the first child of our love, Emily.

CONTENTS

PROLOGUE

I know that we live in an age where the homely or psychological detail is considered all-important. We like heroes in shirtsleeves, or, in other words, we don't like heroes. But things were not always that way, and today is not forever.

—Louis Auchincloss

I

A college president I know keeps three books on his night table: the Bible, the Iliad, and Louis Auchincloss' 1964 novel *The Rector of Justin.* When I once asked him, "Why the novel?," he responded, "Because it raises questions I cannot answer or ignore, the sort of questions that possess a wisdom apart from answers."

In the novel, Dr. Frank Prescott, the eventual founder and rector of Justin Martyr, sets out to build a school that not only trains young men to compete in a ruthless world but compels them to look beyond the present (and the palpable) when charting their ambitions, and challenges them to lay down their lives in the service of a self-transcending ideal. Prescott's dream, no mere nine-teenth-century show of "rugged individualism" or "muscular Christianity," embodies the teacher's ancient and perennial desire to connect the wisdom of the past with man's present and future actions: to educate the young to know what is good, to serve it above self, to reproduce it, and to recognize that in knowledge lies this responsibility. But Prescott fails. Justin Martyr refuses to produce uniform paragons of manly virtue, and Auchincloss leaves his readers to ponder some disturbing questions: Is Prescott's failure inevitable — a flaw of conception, personality, or circumstance? What does his failure teach about the devastating influence of a materialistic and democratic society on education?

1

What is the solution to the paradox between educating for the world's fight and for the soul's salvation?

From a modern reader's point of view, there is something curiously quaint about Headmaster Prescott's concerns. To be sure, *the world's fight* and *the soul's salvation* are supposed to be timeless themes, but within the context of contemporary literature on education, they sound like the wailing of a flute in the Phrygian mode, antiquated and foreign. The new literature plays a very different tune. It reports the influences of applied social research (costing billions of dollars) on educational policy, and it debates the pros and cons of citizen participation in educational policy making. Since 1969, the federal government has spent roughly $70 million a year on national social policy experimentation relating to education alone, according to Cohen and Garet (1975) of Harvard. One is not surprised to find, therefore, that such lucrative stakes invite a preoccupation with these topics, while spawning an army of writers who are more apt to regard themselves as researchers and scientists than as essayists or philosophers or veteran teachers. There is no room in the elaborate federal grant scheme for a Montaigne, a Kant, or a Van Doren. This research into *timely* issues affecting our schools and children has supplanted the *timeless* concerns of the older writers, and in the process, much of the debate over educational policy has centered around how our policy is formulated rather than around what it is or should be.

A new language, turgid and unreadable, hides, under the mantle of experimentation and research, the volumes of common sense cloaked in gibberish now being written by many educational experts. Not only does their language make abominable prose, but it helps to suppress many of the really interesting questions involving value judgments, cultural norms, and religious truths, as well as questions touching on first and final causes and those arising from the marvelous, the transcendent, or the simple craving for justice and goodness. These questions, to borrow a phrase, cannot be put into the language of the computer. When the language of the computer is all one speaks, however, they magically and conveniently disappear.

Unfortunately, this new language seems to inspire reverence and awe in the average citizen, while it permits the expert to stray without public censure from the well-beaten path of his forebears. Even when a confused citizen wonders aloud whether the expert is truly clothed, it hardly matters. The expert's total reliance upon the methods of science renders him incapable of learning from his forebears anyway, for they cannot provide him with the hard statistical and clinical data alone with which he can work. He is like the raw ensign on the bridge of a ship who, mesmerized by the radar scope, refuses to consult an experienced navigator in the fog. His revision of language and his ignorance of history afford him the comfortable delusion of not having to look back to get his bearings. Sure of the all-sufficiency of his methods and blind to many of his own primary assumptions, he rejects charts that were made — he is convinced — by worse navigators than himself, by which he means by navigators whose methods antedate his own.

Meanwhile, in a language all too comprehensible, the journalist decries the nation's plummeting academic standards, Johnny's inability to read and write, the weakness of our science and mathematics programs in comparison with other modern states, the gradual extinction of foreign languages and fine arts from the average high school curriculum, and the scandal of our declining national test scores. As if this were not enough, the journalist goes on to describe the modern American schoolhouse as a breeding ground for various forms of addiction, intimidation, and malaise. But here he leaves off, and the question of what our schools are actually teaching goes back to the expert, the social scientist whose expensive research has done apparently little to improve the situation. When stirred to respond to these charges, the expert may suggest an administrative reorganization or a revised (by which he means simply more) professional training for teachers. He may champion some new-fangled psychological or technological trend or innovation. He may bow to the public's mounting paranoia by demanding a return to the "basics," which when examined turns out to be nothing but utilitarian learning, what the kids need to know to get jobs — the three R's plain and simple. Auchincloss' questions go unanswered, as if they had never been asked or have suddenly lost all meaning. Materialism and democracy no longer appear to threaten education, nor is the soul's salvation a legitimate concern of the modern schoolteacher.

But things were not always this way. The questions and concerns of the older writers were once the focus of education, an education we might rather loosely refer to as *classical.* My purpose in writing this book is to offer a personal interpretation of classical education — its ends, as well as some of its means — and to respond to the objections of those who might approve of the goals of such an education, but who believe that it cannot meet the needs of an industrial democracy or that it is not feasible as a model for mass education. I have some hard words for those social scientists whose analytical methods and unexamined assumptions have worked a profound mischief in our schools. My wish is not, however, to banish science from the modern curriculum, but to save it. For I fear that the modern educator's inchoate understanding of science, his naive belief in its all-sufficiency, and his unwillingness to acknowledge its methodological limitations are leading to a reaction and revulsion against it. If descriptive science is to aid our schools and flourish in them, it must remain in the service of a prescriptive ideal.

II

Education at every level reflects our primary assumptions about the nature of man, and for this reason, no education is innocent of an attitude toward man and his purposes. The writer on education who fails to state his view of man at the outset expects to perform some polemical magic. He masks his premises and invites a gullible reader to judge his conclusions on the deceptive merit of a logical deduction. In fact, whether he wishes to or not, he presupposes an order of human values; his understanding of the nature and proper end of man determines the purposes and tasks that he assigns to education.

What is man, and what are his purposes? The record of man's study of himself suggests answers falling into two broad categories: the prescriptive and the descriptive. The early record favored a prescriptive understanding of man embodied in myths — what Freud (1966-74) shrugged off as "the distorted residue of the wish-phantasies of whole nations." Myths, whether they sang of the exploits of demigods or of heroes, caught in their perpetual flames a unifying vision and standard of man, an Ideal Type striding between the poles of human strength and human frailty.

This Ideal Type was at once immutable yet ever in need of refinement. It was the metaphorical incarnation of wisdom and truth, empowered by education to metamorphose the diligent student. Both an elaborate dogma and a man, it defied comparison with any man, yet all men discovered themselves in it. The Ideal Type embraced Gilgamesh's love for Enkidu and David's love for Jonathan, Odysseus risking his precarious safety to hurl gratuitous insults at the Cyclops, and Achilles deciding at the dawn of human history to die at the supreme moment of glory rather than to live through the long, wizening, connubial years. What made these stories valuable was not their historical authenticity or experimental demonstrability, but their allegiance to a pattern of truth. Whatever fit this pattern was retained and added to the education of future generations. What fell outside this pattern was judged superfluous to the education of the young. But, withal, let my teacher remember to what end his instructions are principally directed, remonstrates Montaigne (1933):

> That he imprint not so much in his schollers mind the date of the ruine of Carthage, as the manners of Hanniball and Scipio, nor so much where Marcellus died, as because he was unworthy of his devoire (duty) he died there: that he teach him not so much to know Histories, as to judge of them. . . . To some kind of men, it is a meere gramaticall studie, but to others a perfect anatomie of Philosophie; but (by) meanes whereof, the secretest part of our nature is searched-into.

When our forebears asked — What is man? — they did not expect a detailed examination of some Saturday morning shopper, Mr. John Q. Public, snatched at random from the crowded *agora* and forced under a microscope or onto a psychiatrist's couch. Nor did they want a statistical analysis of some cross-section of the *demos* for an answer. Of what good to sound learning is a man who looks like every man but in whom no man sees himself? The only use for such analyses, as our modern era shows, is in various forms of exploitation. Statistical man makes a useful abstraction for advertisers and propagandists.

By insisting upon descriptions conforming to a prescriptive pattern of truth, our cultural forebears made art and language the midwives of sound learning, while behaving, to our enlightened eyes, like tribal doctors intent on making the disease match their cure. They never hesitated to prescribe good manners and proscribe bad taste by falsifying the infallible proofs of their five senses. Fabricated descriptions, mere imaginative inventions in homage to the Ideal Type, served the chief aim of their education: *imitatio Christi*, the incarnation of a metaphor.

At the Roman funeral, according to Polybius (1960), this incarnation went so far as to include the dead, who, as honored ancestors, were represented by men of like stature and carriage wearing masks (that resembled them). On the occasion of an illustrious man's death, his grown-up son would mount the rostrum and discourse on the virtues and successful achievements of his father, after which he would recount the successes and exploits of those ancestors whose images were present, beginning with the most ancient.

> By this means, by this constant renewal of the good report of brave men, the celebrity of those who performed noble deeds is rendered immortal, while at the same time the fame of those who did good service to their country becomes known to the people and a heritage for future generations. But the most important result is that young men are thus inspired to endure every suffering for the public welfare in the hope of winning the glory that attends on brave men.

To prove his point, Polybius cites Horatius Cocles, who, after having single-handedly defended Rome from an invader on the far side of the Tiber, plunged in full armor into the river, deliberately sacrificing his life, "regarding the safety of his country and the glory which in future would attach to his name as of more importance than his present existence and the years of life which remained to him." (Alas for Polybius, Livy tells us that Horatius swam across and was saved to face the long, wizening, connubial years.)

Now, the modern educator is apt to dismiss prevarications told in deference to an Ideal Type, while he condemns the arbitrariness of a prescriptive understanding of man. He presumes to have found a method for replacing it, at least initially, with a descriptive understanding. The transition from prescriptive to descriptive definitions of man and his purposes may be chaotic, but with revolutionary fervor, the social scientist affirms the world-transforming benefits of his "new" methods. Yet he seems not to know or to care that his methods were probably familiar to Thales and are at least as old as Hippocrates. Nor does he wonder why the ancients were not so eager as he to substitute late-model scientific knowledge for the junk heap of accumulated wisdom. So, without much sober reflection, the early record is quietly dismissed as unscientific — therefore, error-ridden and useless. In its place, the educator erects a sort of science without reason, random induction predicated upon gnomic utterances like those of Marshall McLuhan: "Data accumulation leads to pattern recognition."

Because it lies beyond the purpose of this prologue to explore the scientific temper of antiquity, I shall only point out that the ancients, unlike us, expected science to enhance their understanding of the material world without partic-ularly helping them to transform it. Their real interest was man, and wherever possible, they tried to turn science away from matter to man. They accepted the material world as they found it and generally regarded schemes to alter the earth's configuration, like Xerxes' canal digging in Thrace, as acts of overween-ing arrogance. Among themselves, they would have agreed that of all creation, the unstable creature man most needed transformation. Thus, Democritus' theory of atomic structures did not start a scientific revolution in physics, but it did provide a theoretical basis for the Epicurean philosophy of life. Thus, Pythagoras, the father of modern mathematics, believed in the power of his discipline to transform man, not matter, through a mathematical (or was it mystical?) communion with nature.

Because the ancients regarded man as free – to the extent his politics and behavior allowed – and not as determined by a material universe, there was little reason to turn science and mathematics into tools with which to mold nonliving matter and man's future. Homer (Fitzgerald 1963) spoke for two thousand years of human experience when he sang:

My word, how mortals take the gods to task!
All their afflictions come from us, we hear.
And what of their own failings? Greed and folly
    double the suffering in the lot of man.

Thus did antiquity's blind mentor reject a naturalistic explanation for man's sufferings. Like the Job and Jeremiah of another tradition, he held fast to a conviction that the evil in nature is unavoidable, but the evil in man is not. Man is helpless to change things for the better, to improve on nature, so long as he himself remains unchanged. "The heart is deceitful above all things, and desper-ately wicked," wrote Jeremiah, "Who can know it?" How the poets and prophets of old would have ridiculed the attempt to lay the blame for man's folly on nature. How they would have warned against tampering with nature in order to correct the human flaw. Such misplaced priorities can only lead to mental confusion, physical destruction, and spiritual damnation.

But modern science – a phrase we can scarcely utter without wedding it to technology – ignores these old warnings. It would change the world and, if we accept the dominant ideological creeds of the nineteenth century, it would change man. Hegel, Comte, Marx, Darwin, Freud – each in his own way identi-fied the sources of evil in *things* outside man or beyond his control. Each depicted the deterministic affect of these external conditions upon man, his language, his thought, his numinous arts, and his sacred beliefs. Ironically, the ideological creeds gave rise to a soaring optimism, a conviction of progress, which soon translated itself into a new educational objective: if you would change man, educate him to the knowledge of how he can change his material conditions. A fundamentally political ideology dedicated to the reform or the anticipated progress of material conditions uprooted the ancient insistence upon a personal ideal.

To understand this change in attitude more fully, consider the positivist influence of the nineteenth-century ideologies upon our thinking about the past and its educational wisdom. The popular historian Will Durant (1953) illustrates this influence when he writes about the Renaissance:

> The medieval love of beauty had matured into magnificent art; but there had been little medieval love of truth to grow into science; and the recovery of ancient literature stimulated a skeptical epicureanism idealizing antiquity rather than a stoic devotion to scientific research aiming to mold the future.

This simple if elaborate summary tells us more about the attitude of the modern historian than about the state of learning during the Renaissance. The equation of truth with science is peculiarly modern, as is the assumption that the science of the ancients desired to be turned into a technology "aiming to mold the future." Yet only if man, like the lizard, takes his markings exclusively from his environment, free from any universal, prescriptive imperatives, can he be so radically changed and his future molded by a technological reconstruction of the material universe. Only when all realities converge on the present and the palpable can truth be exclusively identified with science.

Despite the uncertainties inherent in these prerequisites, the modern world takes considerable pride in having smashed the prescriptive pattern of truth represented by the Ideal Type. Patterns, to be sure, tend to be binding and selective; they may even be accused of making aristocratic or undemocratic demands on the individual. One must weigh, too, the blessings to society and to the individual of the ancient pattern's evolving and integrating vision against the danger that something truly important and necessary for mankind will be excluded from the pattern, ignored because it has no place in the design.

But patterns in learning are inescapable, even if those patterns are wild, random scrawls or are disguised by a pervasive method. The modern school, for example, has an established methodology of which it is more or less unconscious. Its method narrows the search for truth and the free exchange of wisdom by rejecting immaterial categories of thought, as well as the ancient notion of the mind's participation in the object of perception. This method stamps students for life, establishing aprioric rules for perception, thought, and experience and inviting them to dismiss subconsciously the impalpable, the marvelous, the inexplicable. Essentially, it is a method uneasy about life's monumental, problematic concerns — a method that puts these aside, distrusts them. Its rules of analysis increasingly govern our understanding and appreciation of art, poetry, history, and even religion. It effectively excludes the normative aspects of all knowledge (the inquiry concerning what *ought* to be done) in favor of the operational (the inquiry concerning what *can* be done). It shuns the prescriptive in favor of the descriptive.

The first premise of classical education is that the Ideal Type's ancient, prescriptive pattern of truth — which served Christian and Jew, Roman and Greek — remains the most durable and the most comprehensive. The modern affectation for pattern breaking is a bit of educational tomfoolery — a fashionable intellectual fatalism that denies all transcendent value in learning and plays into the hands of utilitarians and other ideologues whose positivism methodically excludes from any emerging patterns a great store of human wisdom and truth, while buying off man's freedom by excusing him from responsibility for what he knows. After all, if he can only be described as a reflex of positive factors, how can man be free and receive praise or blame for his thoughts and actions? To function efficiently becomes his only goal in learning, and the questions — What is man and what are his purposes? — receive as many undifferentiated answers as there are men. Perhaps this is another reason why the modern educator must avoid such questions.

III

The modern era cannot be bothered with finding new answers to old questions like: What is man and what are his purposes? Rather, it demands of its schools: How can modern man better get along in this complicated modern world? *Getting along* — far from suggesting any sort of Socratic self-knowledge or stoical self-restraint — implies the mastery of increasingly sophisticated methods of control over the environment and over others. Man's lust for power, not truth, feeds modern education. But this fact does not worry the educator. From his point of view, the new question has several advantages over the old, the most notable being that it better suits his scientific problem-solving approach. Like the ancient Sophist, he is out to build his status by proving his usefulness; and like the Sophist, he appears unabashedly confident in the efficacy of his methods, which in a peculiar way bestow upon him the power to bestow power.

The abandonment of the normative question for the operational — *ought* for *can* — was predictable. Since the Enlightenment, education has developed an acute case of schizophrenia. Its antipathetic selves have fought over the question of man's identity, the old self asserting a knowledge of man derived from the transcendent ideas and inherited truths of religion, art, and letters, and the new self insisting that man can know himself only by examining the composition of the material universe and drawing his inferences from that. At times, in the poetry of Blake or in the music of Beethoven perhaps, the old self seemed irrepressible; but at last, most of these deviant spiritual influences have been analytically exorcised from the curriculum. In education, as in life, the temptation is to do most what we do best: to adopt, when we are free to do so, the successful and active self and to shuck off the problematic and brooding self. The dramatic successes of the natural sciences each day effect this cure, not only by hypothesizing a new identity for man, but by converting the worrisome old questions — What is man and what are his purposes? — into something the methods of science can without the torment of self-doubt resolve — How can modern man better get along in this complicated modern world?.

Early in this century Alfred North Whitehead (1929) praised the "new" method for breaking the patterns of the old civilization. But in so doing, he contributed to the habit of self-deception and distortion that colors so much of today's thinking about ourselves and our forebears.

The greatest invention of the nineteenth century was the invention of a method of invention. A new method entered into life. In order to understand our epoch, we can neglect all the details of change, such as railways, telegraphs, radios, spinning machines, synthetic dyes. We must concentrate on the method itself; that is the real novelty, which has broken up the foundations of the old civilization. The prophecy of Francis Bacon has now been fulfilled; and man, who at times dreamt of himself as a little lower than the angels, has submitted to become the servant and the minister of nature. It still remains to be seen whether the same actor can play both parts.

The modesty of the great philosopher is as disarming as it is misleading. His remark assumes about the old civilization an exalted self-concept, much as it is often taken for granted that medieval man, who placed his world at the center of a Ptolemaic universe, saw himself seated at God's right hand. Nothing could be more at odds with the truth. Medieval man plowed his feudal fields in the certain knowledge that he toiled at the imperfect fringes of God's handiwork. An outsider, when he looked up, he looked in at the Divine Substance an incalculable distance away. It was left for modern man to cast himself as an insider gazing out at the night heavens.

To be a little lower than the angels was not so much a dream, as Whitehead would have it, as a high calling to hard service. Neither Jew nor gentile, Greek nor barbarian, Christian nor pagan was left much choice other than service. Man served the state or he served himself; he served his higher nature or he served his lower nature; he served God or he served Mammon. His freedom was often defined as a fraction, with service in the numerator. Thus did the King of Israel cry unto his God:

O Lord, truly I am thy servant;
I am thy servant, and the son of thine handmaid;
Thou hast loosed my bonds.

Classical education cast our cultural forebear in the servant's role, warning him in myths, parables, proverbs, histories, laws, and philosophies against hankering after a more exalted part. Any education that might fire in him unworthy ambitions deserved and received censure as foolish and irresponsible. But if the ambition to rule nature and others is deemed unworthy and if its educational encouragement is foolish and irresponsible, these are also the very hallmarks of modern learning: the essential temptation of science's wonderful — but hardly new — method of invention.

Perhaps we are beginning to recognize that Whitehead miscast modern man even more flagrantly than the angel-dreamer of the old civilization. No doubt Bacon, who disparaged classical science for its pure, nontechnological approach, is the true prophet of our age. But Whitehead misrepresents Bacon too. Sir Francis did not prophesy man ministering to the needs of nature. His time machine carried him into a future when man governed nature, mastering her through technology for his own ends. What were those ends? Sir Francis still had enough of the old civilization in him to ask, but he did not stop on his exhilarating journey to wonder who the master would be — Prospero or Faust, Gandhi or Hitler? The past's comment on Bacon's inauspicious augury is a simple lamentation (*New English Bible* 1976):

> Servants have ruled over us: there is none that doth deliver us out
> of their hand.

In our eagerness to solve the material deficiencies of the old civilization, we imported into our schools a method as humble as the English sparrow — simple analysis — but now, the immensity of our success threatens with Toynbeean predictability to overwhelm us. Like the thinker whose brilliance we universally acclaim, Alfred North Whitehead, we have cultivated a perverse form of modesty and self-deception that, in the absence of dogma (the working yet scientifically undemonstrable hypotheses of the old civilization), has allowed us to forget who we are and what our purposes are, as well as to neglect to teach these lessons to our children. We have advocated selfish and irresponsible learning and fostered a system of education that must lead this generation of students — unless the neglected wisdom of the ages is as inconsequential as we seem to think it is — into a sure and speedy disaster.

This point was borne home on me with particular force recently. The science chairman at a well-known New England independent school told me in a voice full of exasperation:

> To pass the standardized tests in biology my students must memorize results of unobserved experiments and know conclusions based upon unpredicated assumptions and unknown methodologies. This year I spent only three weeks on man, and every bit of it was chemistry. There is simply no time to ask: What is the human value and moral implication of all this? How does this touch our lives and increase our understanding of ourselves and of our purposes?

Indeed, it is my intention in this book to ponder the difference between the man who was educated to believe himself to be a little lower than the angels and the man whose education permits him to ignore both angels and God, to avoid knowledge not of the five senses, and to presume mastery over nature but not over himself.

IV

Modern man's inveterate tendency to supplant the normative with the operational — to ask, What *can* be done? instead of, What *ought* to be done? — characterizes today's educational policies. Whereas the normative threatens to lead the student up a steep and rocky ascent toward a self-transforming ideal, the operational looks out on gentle rolling hills and offers a conveyance, the all-conquering methods of science, to carry him about. The administration of the modern school replaces the headmaster of the old and brings with it a whole trainload of technical baggage for finding out what can be done — graphs, charts, statistics, feasibility studies — but precious little imagination of the sort that knows what ought to be done. Its utilitarian and nonnormative program of study stresses freedom at the expense of self-discipline and know-how at the expense of knowledge.

If this is true, one will expect to find this tendency in many areas of modern life. One does. Perhaps the most dramatic illustration of this tendency surfaced during the U.S. war in Vietnam. Many of the missteps taken in education correspond with ironic precision to certain attitudes that became fashionable in the Washington of the early 1960s. The New Frontier slogan captured and popularized these attitudes, including the huge hope that our new technological genius would tame the wild west of distributive inequity and material deficiency. A nation whose schoolchildren had not communed with the spirit of Thucydides presumed to play the part of Athens. Bored with its interminable Cold War against totalitarian Sparta, the young democracy forsook the cautious wisdom of Pericles and embraced the flashy know-how of a young and handsome Alcibiades. It decided to commit itself to fight in Southeast Asia largely because it possessed the infallible technique of "counterinsurgency." (Who in Athens on the day Nicias spoke lacked faith in the trireme's ability to conquer Syracuse?) Only later did the American Athens discover the deadly cost of supplanting the normative with the operational, of allowing what-can-be-done to govern what-ought-to-be-done.

Just as counterinsurgency became a highly sophisticated technique before anyone realized its irrelevance and long after it had manifest a crippling effect on the American psyche, so "educational science" works a similar mischief in our schools by substituting its techniques for a wise and learned imagination. Even by its own objective testing standards, it confesses a failure that only begins to describe the blighted psyche of our young. Declining verbal scores, for instance, not only indicate a failing in communication skills, but a growing inability and unwillingness to think reasonably and to carry on an intelligent dialogue with the past. Unfortunately, the educational establishment lacks the ruthless advantages of the military, where (at least theoretically) the white heat of battle forces error into the open and exposes the incompetency and unimaginativeness of those whose leadership amounts to no more than a vested interest.

Nor is the renewed emphasis upon communication skills enough. Why are these skills important? What is valuable about the traditional means of acquiring these skills through orderly instruction and constant reading and writing? The modern school gives the impression that communication skills are merely techniques whose mastery is important for scoring high on tests and doing well on the job. But is there no transcendent value in learning how to speak and write exactly? To what extent can man be a sentient, moral creature without the ability to communicate clearly with others and with his cultural past? Can there be true independence of thought without mastery of language? In what way is man's verbal ineptitude a barrier to his knowledge of himself and of the world and of what lies beyond the reach of his five senses? What is the connection between how a man thinks and how he acts? Is it possible for man to be cruel, selfish, and barbaric out of an ignorance bred of illiteracy? Modern education's reliance on technique causes these questions to seem irrelevant to the teaching of communication skills. One must wonder, however, if we have not somehow outsmarted ourselves by allowing utilitarian ends to replace the less obvious personal and transcendent ideals of classical education.

In his book *The Best and the Brightest* (1972), David Halberstam warns against the pride and blindness that operational brilliance is heir to. He portrays a presidential cabinet of intellectual technicians who are not able to let go of an idea: men without a dogma or a dialectic, men without the humility of responsible learning, who are quick to put their theories into practice but slow to recognize and remedy their theories' deficiencies. The techniques of these "whiz kids" persisted and bred malpractices of appalling magnitude in Vietnam. Their faith in counterinsurgency illustrates the double danger of any new technique. First, it tends to dissociate itself from the problems and presumptions that called it into being. Like Frankenstein's monster, technique grows a "mind" of its own, a life-system supported by a whole battery of dependent technicians — and it seeks to perpetuate itself long after having served (or perverted) its original purposes. Second, technique tends to exercise a magnetic influence on policy, drawing policy after it, whether that policy is the lofty goal of preserving freedom at home and security abroad or the transcendent value of teaching kids to read and write simple, noble English sentences. The mind of the policy maker, unaccustomed to abstract, dialectical thought and seldom imbued with an imaginative sense of responsibility toward the past, prefers to grab onto a concrete operational means rather than to feel the way tentatively toward an abstract normative end. Both policy maker as strategist and school administrator as educator resemble the farmer who tries to plow a field with his eyes on the plow rather than on that imaginary point on the horizon on which he must fix his gaze if he expects to leave a straight furrow.

As it affects education, this fixation with technique to the detriment of the task is especially pernicious. For when we accept the tyranny of the real over the ideal, we deny the human spirit — the better half of learning and the better half of man. Instead, we concentrate on his Caliban half, making him a more efficient berry gatherer, a more discriminating shell collector, or a more willing water carrier. The notion of spirit we dismiss as mythological, out-of-date, and irrelevant; at any rate, the fact that it cannot be seen in space or under a microscope makes it, in the end, no longer a proper subject for instruction. Yet our very mania for technology, our determination to transform the material universe, argues that the world is not good enough for the human spirit to accept.

Our fascination with technical means, by the very nature of things, subverts the supreme task of education — the cultivation of the human spirit: to teach the young to know what is good, to serve it above self, to reproduce it, and to recognize that in knowledge lies this responsibility. Short of accomplishing this task, the training in our schools must seem purposeless, except in the narrow utilitarian sense of serving "natural religion": that is, the individual's lust for power, sex, and status. Democratic and materialistic society are quite sufficient, without the aid of our schools, for educating the young in the rites of natural religion. Moreover, although the modern school indoctrinates its inmates to think otherwise, one can live without the ability to make operational analyses; but normative inquiry is a vital function of all human life. Without it, as Northrop Frye (1974) writes in his treatise on William Blake, we are left with only "our verminous crawling egos that spend all their time either wronging others or brooding over wrongs done to them. The end of all natural religion, however well-meaning and good-natured, is corrupt and decadent society rolling downhill to stampeding mass hysteria and maniacal warfare."

The good school does not just offer what the student or the parent or the state desires, but it says something about what these three ought to desire. A school is fundamentally a normative, not a utilitarian, institution, governed by the wise, not by the many. It judges man as an end, not as a means; it cultivates the human spirit by presenting a complete vision of man as he lives and as he ought to live in all his domains — the individual, the social, and the religious. It teaches the student how to fulfill his obligations to himself, to his fellow man, and to God and His creation. Its understanding of man, therefore, is prescriptive — and its curriculum and organization allegorize the scope, the sequence, and the vision that all men must recognize and accept as fundamental if they hope to grow to their full human stature.

The need for a prescriptive understanding of man suggests that we make a retrospective beginning. The rebirth of the old is not incommensurate with the new. "For century after century, almost without interruption," wrote Ortega y Gasset (1975),

> whenever European culture needed an ideal, it always found it in the culture of Greece. Remember that what is innermost in a culture, most

productive, the force that fashions it and drives everything else is a repertoire of longings, norms, of *desiderata* — in short, its ideal.

During the Italian Renaissance, the rediscovery of Greece's longings and norms, of its Ideal Type, was accompanied by vast social changes and brilliant new discoveries, as well as by a renewed sense of human worth and potential. Classical education refreshes itself at cisterns of learning dug long ago, drawing from springs too deep for taint the strength to turn our cultural retreat into advance.

PART I

THE IDEA OF
A CLASSICAL EDUCATION

1

VIRTUE IS THE FRUIT OF LEARNING

I come from the Town of Stupidity; it lieth about four degrees beyond the City of Destruction.

—John Bunyan

I

The popular mind associates the idea of a classical education with the narrow and elitist schools of Victorian England. In fact, these schools perverted classical education by teaching in precept and in example a hereditary aristocratic ideal intended to serve the ambitions of Empire and to preserve the status quo. In 1867, the average Englishman was just receiving the franchise and a precarious seat on the middle-class coach. To him, classical education meant little more than a symbol of ruling class privilege and a study of Latin, with perhaps a smattering of Greek. The century's growing class consciousness and emerging ideological creeds, the failure of its classicists to teach normatively, and the state's waking involvement in education further blurred the public's image of classical learning. By the turn of the century, a growing number of self-proclaimed progressives, desiring to democratize the school and mistaking what went on in Victorian schools with classical education, began to put forward their own theories on education. In the United States, John Dewey (Karp 1980) called for schools adapted "to the circumstances, needs, and opportunities of industrial civilization"; and William James (1978) demanded "truth's cash-value in experiential terms" — a test designed to flunk the classical prototype. Neither ideal types, aprioric truths, nor transcendent human needs figure in the writings of these spokesmen for the progressive movement. But to the extent that the Victorian schoolmaster perverted classical learning and the progressive educator ignored it, our modern schools have suffered.

17

Classical education is not, preeminently, of a specific time or place. It stands instead for a spirit of inquiry and a form of instruction concerned with the development of style through language and of conscience through myth. The key word here is *inquiry*. Everything springs from the special nature of the inquiry. The inquiry dictates the form of instruction and establishes the moral framework for thought and action. Classical inquiry possesses three essential attributes. The first of these is a general curiosity, as opposed to the systematic or specific interest of modern science. One does not launch a classical inquiry with a preconceived methodology or from the point of view of an established academic discipline. Consequently, the field is open for all sorts of questions, whether regarding the nature of true happiness, the cause of the Persian wars, or the source of the Nile. Second, one responds to these questions by forming imaginative hypotheses. The very nature of the questions, being far-flung and wide-ranging, often makes impossible what qualify today as scientific hypotheses. Third, one completes the inquiry by devising methods for testing the hypotheses. Again, the restrictions placed by modern science upon methodology are not adequate. The method used to test the hypothesis formed in a classical inquiry may involve reason or observation, logic or experimentation. The inquirer may even seek confirmation for his hypothesis in an emotional or religious experience. How else, ultimately, does one test the value of a poem or the validity of God's love?

General curiosity, imagination in forming hypotheses, and method in testing them, then, mark the classical spirit of inquiry. This bent of mind allows the educated man to go on educating himself or extending the realms of knowledge for his fellows. In the process of asking a wide range of questions, of forming hypotheses, and of testing their consistency with known facts, the student learns about the nature of his subject and about the methods appropriate for mastering it. This process — because it is the indispensable tool for unearthing all human knowledge — is the only true basis for a classical, or universal, education. Only the person whose mental habits conform to this generous process can be said to be "educated" in a universal sense. This is the person who, as Aristotle (1961) writes in his essay *On the Parts of Animals,* "should be able to form a fair off-hand judgment as to the goodness or badness of the method used by a professor in his exposition." This is the person competent to judge what the experts say without being an expert himself.

The desire to inculcate such a spirit of inquiry in the young dictates the form of instruction. Just as inquiry is prerequisite for the attainment of knowledge, form is the necessary precondition for all experience and expression, perception and comprehension. The mind rejects formlessness; nature will not tolerate a void. To impart the spirit of inquiry, therefore, and to clarify the objects of study, the need arises for a *formal* education in which the curriculum ("the course run") is selected and organized in accordance with criteria supporting the nature of the inquiry being taught. The criteria for the classical curriculum are many, but two deserve our immediate attention. The first of these derives from the tendency of a classical inquiry to rely more heavily on logic than on experimentation. Reason, Aristotle asserted, "forms the starting-point" (Burnet 1976). Whatever lesson or book, topic or investigation enables the student to perceive, articulate, and comprehend reason at work best suits the classical curriculum. Whereas this introduces a principle of exclusiveness based on classical inquiry's preference for logical methods, the second criterion urges that the student's general curiosity be stimulated and that the curriculum include those baggy, baffling, normative questions of style (aesthetics) and conscience (ethics) that slip from the grip of our scientific method. Together, these criteria provide a dialectical core, a living debate, around which the form of instruction takes shape.

Unlike Aristotle, the modern educator looks upon observation, not reason, as the starting point; and he distrusts the classical schoolmaster's tolerance for normative questions and for the use of methods appropriate to such questions, as well as his insistent search for moral content and reasonable form in history, literature, religion, and art. His misgivings stem perhaps from a too lofty regard for the experimentally verifiable or from a lack of sympathy with the goals of the classical teacher, who is not trying to serve up verifiable facts, but is hoping to engrain in his students the wonderful spirit of inquiry. Whatever his reasons for rejecting the classical curriculum, his classrooms suffer from its absence in three notable ways. In them, human experience tends to be dealt with narrowly and reductively, broken down into isolated, unconnected units; students ignorant of what questions to ask are presented with uninvited and consequently meaningless information; and there is no basis for making moral and aesthetic judgments or for attaching learning to behavior.

On the other hand, the classical form of instruction serves a cultural purpose, as well as an intellectual one. It invites the student to adopt for himself his civilization's highest moral and aesthetic values; at the same time, the student learns the rules governing a universal process of inquiry. There is, of course, more than a hint of dogma in any education presuming to pass judgment on the way a person lives and on the way he thinks. Yet a classical education presents the right way, not with the intention of stifling future inquiry, but as a necessary starting point for dialogue. In this sense, dogma can resemble art: it confronts man with some truth about himself, a kind of truth that might have taken him a lifetime of error and misdirection to arrive at for himself, but ultimately, a truth he must test in his own experience of life if he is to appropriate it for himself and benefit from the confrontation.

II

Aristotle is our best introduction to the idea of a classical education. He shares the popular view that a happy, well-adjusted individual is the true end of learning, and he does not shrink from giving a full account of what he means by happiness. Like us, he is without illusions concerning man's craving for happiness and its prerequisites. "Happiness is believed to depend on leisure," he writes, "for the aim of all our business is leisure just as the aim of war is peace" (Burnet 1976). His practical approach to education also resembles ours, making the school a state, or community, concern: the community's formal means of offering its members access to what we and Aristotle like to call "the good life."

Aristotle's practical approach to education derives from his Platonic understanding of knowledge as an activity and from his recognition of the political conditions upon which this activity depends. Plato regarded knowledge neither as a possession of something outside the mind nor as a measurable state of mind, but as a logical process attending the activity of learning. His definition of knowledge as an activity of learning rather than as a condition of having learned is important to the idea of a classical education. To begin with, his definition allows for no analytical separation of knowledge from responsibility. "A condition may exist in us," affirms Aristotle (1975),

> and yet produce no good result, as in the case of a man who is asleep or in a state of inactivity from any other cause. But this cannot be the case with an activity; it will of necessity produce action and good action. In the Olympian Games it is not the handsomest and strongest that win the crown, but those who actually compete; for it is some of these that are victorious. In the same way, those who win the fine things of life are those who act aright.

The purpose of education is not the assimilation of facts or the retention of information, but the habituation of the mind and body to will and act in accordance with what one knows.

Since knowledge is an activity and all activities have ends — one studies engineering to build bridges, one builds bridges to speed transit, one speeds transit to accomplish certain commercial or military goals, and so on — knowledge must also have an end. What is that end? According to Aristotle, the perfect end of education will be an activity that is engaged in for its own sake, complete and sufficient unto itself. Aristotle calls the activity for which education prepares man — happiness. So far, all might agree. But as to the nature of happiness, the opinion of mankind is divided into at least three ways. Many believe that happiness attends the life of pleasure; others credit the practical life with producing happiness; but the wise — Aristotle has no doubt — find it in the theoretic life.

The life of pleasure eventually evades and exasperates the pleasure seeker because it is not a life sufficient unto itself. Pleasure demands a never-ending list of luxurious accessories, the acquisition of which wears man down with work and worry. In the end, the pleasure seeker becomes preoccupied with what he lacks to complete his picture of happiness: gratification never catches up with his desire, and consumption consumes the consumer. By the same token, the practical life falls short of completeness. The wealth one acquires in business is a useful thing, but as such, it exists for the sake of something else. The honor accruing to the just politician is a worthy reward, but it "depends more on the people who give it than on the man to whom it is given" (Aristotle 1975). Happiness must be something that belongs to a person and cannot be snatched from him at the whim of the *demos.*

So we arrive at the theoretic life — not to be confused, as Professor Burnet (1976) warns, with the contemplative or passive life.

> What Aristotle calls *theoria* is emphatically an activity. The fact is that he includes a good many things in it which we are too apt to regard as wholly different, things of which we fail to realize as he did the fundamental identity. In the first place, scientific research is *theoria,* and no doubt Aristotle was thinking chiefly of that. But so too is the artist's life, so far as he is not a mere artificer, and so is all enjoyment of art and literature. So too is the life of the religious man who sees all things in God.

Aristotle defends the theoretic life as the true end of education and the source of happiness. One does not require more than the bare necessities of life to achieve happiness in thought, nor is the active life of the mind dependent upon the inherently unequal endowments of nature. One need be neither strong nor handsome, well-born nor gregarious, nay, not even brilliant to participate happily in the theoretic life. The theoretic life completes the individual, holding him against the warmth of the divine spark in his nature and making sense of an existence otherwise consumed by the infinite wishing of one thing for the sake of another. Indeed, the theoretic life is the life of virtue, so long as we mean by virtue all that the Greek *arete* expresses: the life that knows and reveres, speculates and acts upon the Good, that loves and re-produces the Beautiful, and that pursues excellence and moderation in all things.

This vision of life dedicated to perfecting the self is, remember, from the scientific-tempered Aristotle, not from "that idealistic dreamer, Plato." To be sure, Aristotle recognizes how heavily the individual's ability to practice the life of virtue and to attain happiness hangs upon certain practical conditions, namely, a harmoniously ordered community wherein the necessities of life can be met without difficulty and a public determination to educate every man in the knowledge of how most wisely to invest the considerable leisure time available to him in such a community. But these conditions again are referred back to the school, where education forms in the young a character in harmony with the laws and customs of the community, as well as those habits of mind and body promising the highest return on each leisure moment to both the individual and the community.

"The end of Politics is the highest good," Aristotle (1959) insists, "and there is nothing this science takes so much pains with as producing a certain character in the citizens, that is, making them good and able to do fine actions." The community's obligation to underwrite the conditions for the life of virtue is the basis for Aristotle's political theory, for his and Plato's enormous emphasis upon the character-forming role of the law, and for the concept of the community as an educator — a concept receiving its most eloquent expression in Pericles' Funeral Oration. Only when the community fails to meet these conditions does Aristotle hesitantly relinquish the role of education to smaller groups within the community.

For Aristotle, then, education is an eminently practical and public matter, but not as we today tend to define practical and public matters in utilitarian terms. The life of virtue has nothing to do with one's prospective pleasures, possessions, or practical affairs, but concerns the manner in which one is prepared to spend one's leisure hours. The public interest in the individual's life and learning is not that of a prospective employer or bureaucrat. Although the individual must live in harmony with the community, his life of virtue ought not to be subsumed by the political purposes of the state — for ultimately, the state's only justification is that it makes the good life, the life of virtue, the life that takes responsibility for what it knows, possible. The self-improvement flowing from this life, as pursued passionately in pastimes, redounds to the benefit of the community, the pleasure of the individual, and the true happiness and harmony of both.

III

As Aristotle demonstrates, the Greek achievement in education found its abundant source in Plato's question: Can virtue be taught? Can the knowledge of good, the love of beauty, the vision of greatness, and the passion for excellence be learned in a classroom? No notable or influential ancient, it is fair to say, ever answered this question in the negative. Not even Socrates, the man who raised it, doubted that somehow virtue can be taught and that the teacher's most enviable and essential task is to teach it. Vittorino da Feltre, who restored classical education to Northern Italy in the fifteenth century, attributed this uncontested principle to an obvious fact of life: "Not everyone is obliged to excel in philosophy, medicine, or the law, nor are all equally favored by nature; but all are destined to live in society and to practice virtue" (Origo 1960).

Three centuries later, Samuel Johnson (1958) reiterated da Feltre's conviction:

> The truth is that knowledge of external nature, and the sciences which that knowledge requires or includes, are not the great or the frequent business of the human mind. Whether we provide for action or conversation, whether we wish to be useful or pleasing, the first requisite is the religious and moral knowledge of right and wrong, the next is an

acquaintance with the history of mankind, and with those examples which may be said to embody truth, and prove by events the reasonableness of opinions. Prudence and Justice are virtues and excellences of all times and of all places; we are perpetually moralists, but we are geometricians only by chance.

Thus did Dr. Johnson underscore the unchanging validity of classical education's preoccupation with forming the virtuous man at a time when education seemed destined to turn away from "religious and moral knowledge" into the cold embrace of the "knowledge of external nature." Could he have predicted the day, one wonders, when the "knowledge of external nature" stood in judgment over "religious and moral knowledge" and when geometricians were assumed to have morals peculiar to their trade and class?

Geometry, in Dr. Johnson's typology, symbolizes the practical life, which exercises a considerable power over man without in any way meeting his fundamental human needs. On the eve of England's Industrial Revolution, Dr. Johnson recognized the temptation to make education a preparation for the practical life either by concentrating exclusively on science or by turning all studies into sciences. Predictably, as science took a technological turn and as education began preparing students for work rather than for leisure, for the factory rather than for the parlor, the school itself came to resemble the factory, losing its idiosyncratic, intimate, and moral character. Reacting to "missile gaps" and fluctuating employment figures, the state in the modern era exaggerates this tendency by looking upon the school as a means for supplying the technocrats that society is presumed to need. In its utilitarian haste, the state often peddles preparation for the practical life to our young as the glittering door to the life of pleasure; but by encouraging this selfish approach to learning, the state sows a bitter fruit against that day when the community depends on its younger members to perform charitable acts and to consider arguments above selfish interest. In so behaving, this state threatens the conditions necessary for the life of virtue and weakens its own justification for being.

Although Aristotle's distinction between work and leisure helps to clarify the purposes of education, it is not a distinction that Dr. Johnson finds acceptable in speaking about the life of virtue. Virtue, after all, is not a parlor game, but a perpetual activity, and an education that fails to prepare man for the life of virtue robs him as a youth of his chance to receive what Cicero (Harris et al. 1960) calls "right reason": the ability to recognize who he is and what his purposes are in terms of the virtues and excellences found, though hidden, in nature. Education for the life of virtue instructs man to perceive and to imitate in nature, often through a study of the mimetic arts, letters, and sciences, these embodied truths, making of himself a work of art. "Be always at work carving your own statue," taught Plotinus (Marrou 1964); presumably, Plotinus also taught his students how this work could best be accomplished.

To hold that virtue can be taught and that it is the chief duty of the school to teach it need not imply a belief in the perfectibility of man. Rather, it implies a belief in the ideal of virtue, as well as in the value of an education based upon the attempt to know and to emulate this ideal. The ancients admitted no contradiction in this, but our modern operational mood makes this effort much more difficult. Ideals contradict incontrovertible experience, for no one has seen or tested an ideal. Thus, we tend to look upon virtue as what under a specific set of circumstances can be achieved, rather than as what ought to be achieved under all circumstances. We expect from our students what we might call "reasonable behavior," by which we mean whatever makes them sufferable — never mind perfect. Above all, we deny the need for any connection between schoolwork and student behavior, often because no such connection any longer exists — and plummeting results greet our sinking expectations.

IV

Although no one in it seriously challenged the imperative to teach virtue, the classical world divided roughly between philosophers and rhetoricians over the question of *how* virtue is taught. The philosophers looked upon virtue as an inherent property of man's nature, whereas the rhetoricians were of the general opinion that virtue is acquired. Either man is by nature good and becomes corrupted by society or he is born flawed, and society must save him. At bottom, this conflict still rages, but modern science adds an apocalyptic dimension — with Utopian "philosophers" planning for the day when technology permits an equitable and efficient reordering of society, while anti-Utopian "rhetoricians" predict the sinister uses and cataclysmic effects destined to spill from a new technology in the hands of flawed men. In any case, upon this timeless distinction, the philosophers and rhetoricians of antiquity built their theoretical answers to the question: *How* is virtue taught?

Plato, speaking for the philosophers, subscribed to the belief that virtue is a gift from God. To illustrate, he tells Protagoras the charming account of a conversation between Hermes and Zeus. While Zeus is putting the finishing touches on his human creation, Hermes asks him if virtue is to be distributed among men like the gifts of the arts, unequally, with only a favored few receiving skills in medicine and in music. But Zeus resists this proposal and commands Hermes to distribute the gift of virtue to all men equally, "for cities cannot exist if a few only share in the virtues, as in the arts" (Jowett 1969). (Evidently, like Aristotle, Zeus understands the political utility of a virtuous citizenry.)

Later, in the *Meno,* Socrates rationalizes this myth by declaring that the soul is "immortal and having been born again many times, and having seen all things that exist, whether in this world or the world below, has knowledge of them all" (Jowett 1969). From this metaphysical rationalization, Plato derives his theory of innate ideas. To obtain knowledge, therefore, man must uncover those ideas buried in his nature. This he does by thinking consciously with a tool that Plato describes as a "dialectic." Dialectic is simply the form of the activity of thinking: the mind's habit of challenging the thoughts and observations originating inside and outside itself and of engaging in a desultory dialogue with itself until the issues are resolved. By bringing the form of man's mental activity to light, Plato enables man to include others in his dialogue with himself and turns dialectic into an activity of learning (or knowledge). In the hands of a skilled teacher like Socrates, the dialectic can elicit from others a recollection of their innate, hidden ideas. Once thus exposed, these ideas form a pattern of truth (or self-knowledge), liberating and perfecting the individual.

It remains for us to ask what the self-knowledge obtained by eliciting man's innate ideas has got to do with the teaching of virtue. Plato's answer is direct and emphatic: no man knowingly chooses evil. Evil, after all, sooner or later brings pain and destruction — and no one, at least in a Socratic dialogue, knowingly seeks to hurt or destroy himself. Choosing evil, therefore, implies thoughtlessness, that is to say, a mind no longer challenging its opinions and observations, a mind incapable of seeing the deleterious effects of evil. One heals this mind by giving it a dialectical antidote — reawakening the activities of thinking and learning. Once these activities are renewed, the subject will again be able to discern good from evil and will seek to avoid moral or physical pain by refraining from evil acts. The health of his perfect self-knowledge grows into the vigor of moral perfection.

In passing, it is worth noting that although Plato's means of teaching virtue rests upon a theory of innate ideas, the theory of innate ideas commands much broader support than the charming myth and metaphysical rationalization of Socrates. Cicero's writings on natural law contain antiquity's most influential defense of this theory, and down to the present day, men have sought and found reasons for believing in innate ideas. Immanuel Kant wrestled brilliantly with the problem in his inconclusive effort to prove that an "aprioric synthetic proposition" is possible, and Jung broke with Freud over this very question, claiming that consciousness arises from the unconscious rather than from experience. Nor, as the ancient rhetoricians affirmed, must one be a Platonist to answer in the affirmative Hannah Arendt's (1978) timely question: "Could the activity of thinking as such, the habit of examining whatever happens to come to pass or to attract attention, regardless of results and specific content, could this activity be among the conditions that make men abstain from evil-doing or even actually 'condition' them against it?"

The more popular and practical rhetorician doubted the philosopher's ability to make such miraculous cures by eliciting virtue from man's vital core. The philosophical cure, he rightly perceived, depended upon a rare ability to sustain intellectual passion, "to burn always (in Pater's phrase) with a hard, gemlike flame." Without this extraordinary ability, the critical connection between the dialectic and the deed is lost. Aristotle (Burnet 1976) himself concedes this point when he tells his students:

> It is quite right, then, to say that it is by doing just deeds that a just man is made, and that a temperate man is made by acting temperately.

There is not the slightest prospect of anyone being made good by any other process. Most men, indeed, shirk it and take refuge in the theory of goodness. They fancy that they are philosophers, and that this will make them good. But they are really just like people who listen attentively to what their doctor has to say and do not obey one of his prescriptions. There is about as much chance of those who study philosophy in this way gaining health of soul as of such people getting well and strong of body.

Man with his philosophizing is no more virtuous than he is without it — possibly less so, since there is always the danger that his philosophy will lead him to question the grounds for moral action without providing him the answers. These grounds for moral action — the dogma of self-evident and inherited truth and meaning — the rhetorician most desired through his eloquence to preserve and to implant in the hearts of his students.

Whereas Plato recognized beauty in truth, the rhetorician saw truth in beauty; more than that, the rhetorician believed that whenever truth comes to man by way of beauty, it necessarily transforms his character and ennobles his behavior. Virtue, in his view, grows out of the beautiful adornments of dogma, not from the inelegant dialectic of philosophy. Conscience springs from style. "The right word," the great rhetorician Isokrates (Marrou 1964) taught, "is a sure sign of good learning." Learning to speak properly causes the student not only to think but to live properly. "In the eyes of the Ancients," writes Marrou (1964), "eloquence had a truly human value transcending any practical applications . . . it was the one means for handing on everything that made man man, the whole cultural heritage that distinguished civilized men from barbarians. The idea underlies all Greek thought, from Diodorus Siculus to Lianius."

Not only did philosopher and rhetorician share the purpose of teaching virtue, but both borrowed freely from the methods of each other. The philosopher's pretense of scorning style was eloquent indeed, and perhaps no one has ever written with more urgency and acumen on the connection between poetry and right conduct than Plato. The rhetorician, for his part, may not have flaunted a search for truth or professed belief in man's innate goodness, but his learned recitations are everywhere infused with love of truth and with intimations of virtue in his listeners to which he makes appeal. Philosophical and rhetorical learning — as two rival approaches to education — enriched classical culture without disturbing its profound unity. But in the modern era, we watch helplessly as the near lockstep uniformity of state and private education emasculates learning and impoverishes culture. The lesson of the ancient quarrel between philosopher and rhetorician seems unimportant. Do we not understand that conflict which shares its purposes is good and that uniformity does not mean unity any more than conformity signifies independent and intelligent agreement?

So long as the ancient quarrel persisted, it fired both sides with an intellectual passion for learning and helped to personalize, as well as to achieve, the goals of education. Both philosophers and rhetoricians hoped to demonstrate the efficacy of their respective methods by pointing to the virtuous lives of their students. Each side competed for the same prize, the formation of the virtuous man; each directed his opponent's attention to moral ends by attacking the other's tendency to become bogged down with intellectual or utilitarian concerns. With the unchallenged ascendency of the analytical methods of science, however, something of this healthy debate has gone out of modern education, and with it, the excitement of intellectual passion that makes the school a place where virtue can be taught.

2

THE WORD IS TRUTH

There is much in life that is casual, and there is also much that is unusual. The Word is given the sublime right to enhance chance and to make of the transcendental something that is not accidental.

— *Vladimir Nabokov*

I

While establishing his dialectial credentials, Socrates shocked his contemporaries by arguing that virtue and vice are not the inherent properties of objects; they result instead from the rational or irrational use of objects. More incredibly, he taught that it is worse to wrong another than to wrong oneself. Such unorthodox notions seemed to contradict the evidence of human experience, especially as recorded in the myths. The sudden rational articulation of these two propositions concerning the nature of virtue forecast a violent collision between Socrates' dialectical *logos* and the dogmatic *mythos.* To the affects of this collision on education, we now must turn our attention.

Originally, the Greek *logos* meant simply "word," or "the word by which the inward thought is expressed." Perhaps the *mythos* shaped the *logos* in primeval times, molding the first words to the contours of its compelling narrative; but after awhile, as old words appeared in new contexts and took on richer shades of meaning, the *logos* began asserting itself, bringing to each new myth the values and colors of former myths. The discovery of reason attended this phenomenon. However nonrational myths were, they betrayed man's urge to explain what he found in himself and in the world, as well as his belief that explanation was somehow possible. Regardless of how firmly they avowed the inscrutibility of Divine Reason, the early cosmological myths belied a confidence

28

that reason existed and left the way open for man to decipher what reason he could from the puzzling pattern of the gods' behavior. This pattern reflected the myth-maker's insight into the internal and external realities and aided man in developing rules for ordering his thought and behavior in accordance with the immanent reasonableness of these realities.

As reasoning Athena burst from the head of Zeus, the ruling god of mythology, so out of the impulse for myth man distilled reason. *Logos* evolved to signify "the inward thought itself" or "the intrinsic-abstract-rational principle governing all things." Almost immediately, as we see in Plato's *Republic,* reasoning Athena began to criticize her mythological father — although not without a show of deference and a willingness to quote father whenever his authority assisted her argument. This evolution continued into Hellenistic times, when the *logos* attempted to avenge itself on the *mythos* by subsuming it. The guardians of the *mythos,* the teachers of rhetoric, endeavored to extract the rational poltergeist believed to dwell in the body of each myth. They offered every species of scholarly explanation for the perplexing behavior of the gods and heroes — and sometimes presented their explanations as surrogates for the myths themselves. But their plot failed: myth defies analysis, especially in instruction, and happily, usually survives it.

It has become almost commonplace to divide ancient consciousness thus between the *logos* and the *mythos,* but when fully understood, this division is recognized as timeless — a precondition, as it were, of the human mind. No one exists who does not in some measure possess these complementary defenses against an unintelligible and hostile world. The *mythos* represents man's imaginative and, ultimately, spiritual effort to make this world intelligible; the *logos* sets forth his rational attempt to do the same. What is not hedged off in the severely symmetrical German garden of reason belongs to the uncharted wilderness of mythopoeic imagination — well, perhaps not entirely uncharted, for even the most rational man spends most of his life wandering in the wilderness, learning its ways and doing his best to follow whatever rudimentary maps come to hand. John Bunyan, for example, sent his Pilgrim walking through this woolly wilderness with only a Bible to guide him: a testimony to Bunyan's all-encompassing faith in the holy book. Moses descended from Mount Sinai with clay tablets that changed 40 years in the wilderness into a spiritual odyssey.

At the risk of slipping into the ancients' habit of arguing by analogy, the wilderness ordeal vividly illustrates two fundamental laws of the imaginative consciousness bearing on a classical education. The first pertains to the quality of the myth. A good myth, like a good map, enables the wanderer to survive, perhaps even to flourish, in the wilderness. To this end, classical education, like Hebrew education, carefully preserves the best myths within its tradition and insists that each new generation of students learn these myths, imprisoning them in their hearts.

Second, one's chances of survival in a wilderness are greater when one is not alone. This law is no less true in the psychological trials and tribulations of everyday life. In this regard, classical education's emphasis upon the mastery of a common psychological inheritance ensures a social and psychological cohesiveness in the world. Myths provide each member of society with something to dignify and lend coherence to his life, as well as with something of quality he can share with the other members of his community.

Nowadays, our rich mythological inheritance no longer provides social cohesiveness and individual coherence, and modern criticism is obliged to distinguish between the universal myth (or archetype) of almost all art and literature created before the nineteenth century and the personal symbolism of most modern creativity. Curiously, this signal fact is assumed by the modern teacher to render three thousand years of art and literature inaccessible to the student. Instead, students are encouraged to kick around in the private symbolic universes of Yeats, Joyce, and D. H. Lawrence. Can anyone wonder why psychological survival seems so much more difficult in the modern era? Despite the locustlike proliferation of our symbols and ourselves, we wander in a truly uncharted wilderness — and we wander alone, like the poor ghost of Pound in the later *Cantos.*

Myths assure us of more than a healthy psyche. They provide the necessary basis for our civilized acts. Through myth, we see our own feelings refined and given meaning, while we receive confirmation of others' emotions. Consider a passage from the *Song of Songs* (Graves 1973):

> How beautiful you are, my love, how beautiful!
> Your eyes are like a dove's, your hair ripples like a flock of goats bounding down from Mount Gilead. Your teeth are white as a flock of shorn sheep come up from their washing, none of them barren, all mothers of twins.
> Your lips are like scarlet ribbons, your voice is melodious.
> Your cheeks are the color of a ripe pomegranate — save for what lies hidden by your tresses.
> Your neck is straight and strong like the battlemented tower that David built; in it hung a thousand shields, armor for valiant men.
> Your breasts are like twin gazelles browsing among lilies.
> Let me now approach the mountain of myrrh and the hills of frankincense, and there remain until the day breaks and shadows depart.
> You are all beautiful, my love. I find no fault in you.

At our finest moments, we have all known such feelings, but we need the poet to clarify and sustain these moments for us. The poet's admiration for his beloved is without perversion or sentimentality, and his imagery suggests an ennobling and self-transcending sexuality — nothing tawdry, nothing vain. It is not surprising that Hebrew scholars have read the *Song of Songs* as an allegory of love between Jehovah and Israel, or that Christian scholars accept it as a symbolic description of the love of Christ for His Church. For the love the poet expresses, although intensely personal, is also universal and divine. His myth raises human sexuality out of the technical mire of the modern sex manual and imbues it with the significance and loveliness characterizing Dante's (1972): "Love that moves the sun and the other stars."

To the considerable extent that questions of value, of right and wrong, of justice and of beauty cannot be experimentally or rationally resolved, myth allows many individuals to share an epiphany, a vision of truth granting them a basis for accepting certain normative standards for which there are no clear or convincing proofs. The myth of Job, for instance, has helped centuries of men and women endure suffering and injustice in the quiet certainty of right conduct. Job argues for the nonrational human consciousness of an absolute good — of a way that is righteous despite what the reasonable doctrines of Deuteronomic theologians or utilitarian philosophers have to say. Life is full of moral imperatives that defy our reason and our simplistic systems of punishment and reward and our theoretical models of value-preferences. If the basis for each individual's right conduct were *his* test of reasonableness, reason might easily be turned into a tool of self-interest. If the study of myth did not attend a classical inquiry, whose methods for testing hypotheses are not exclusively objective or scientific, subjectivity might undermine the cultural role of the school. But myth assures mankind that certain values transcend reason to give human existence meaning within an unchanging frame of reference, while ensuring unity among the members of the community concerning these values. This unity of values is the hallmark of culture. Without this unity regarding the imponderables, civilized actions become impossible, and man is cast upon the shabby mythology of his own random dream-worlds and is at the mercy of state and natural religions.

The *mythos* is the very skeleton of civilization. Remove it and watch all the flesh of political stability, scientific invention, and social sophistication collapse. Myths, like the panegyrics at a Roman funeral, remind man to think and to act out of a sense of responsibility toward the past. Those who forget the past are bound to be condemned to repeat its mistakes ad infinitum. Myths inspire men to perform great and selfless deeds by assuring and warning them that their actions are not individual, but symbolic. Their actions and ideas have never-ending consequences. Truly, a civilized action or idea assumes the first principle of the *mythos* — that the thought and deed are both determined and existential at the same time, formed by the past, while transforming the future. The student of myths is likewise transformed by participating in them through his imagination. The myth involves and commits him, civilizes him, stamps him. Its transcendent nature, paradoxically, grounds the student in time while animating his eternal soul. Describing the aim of both teacher and student in studying myth, the American poet Hermann Hagedorn (Gable 1977) writes: "To seek to bring the spirit of the dead to life, to summon that spirit to speak and to have it speak, and to make it somehow again a part of the society of the living is an enterprise in which only the imaginative mind can hope to succeed." Caught up in the myth, the student measures his deeds against his dreams, his ambitions against his altruisms, his despair against his faith, and thereby receives a complete vision of himself as he lives in all his domains — the individual, the social, and the religious.

II

Why, then, if myth bears such splendid gifts, does Plato attack it in the *Republic*? The reason, I believe, has nothing to do with the social and individual value of an active *mythos*. Rather, it is only by contrasting reason with myth that Plato can differentiate and clarify the dialectical nature of the *logos*. As between philosophy and rhetoric, the apparent quarrel between *logos* and *mythos* resolves itself in a dialectical unity of opposites. The one cannot maintain its identity and purposes without the other — no more than a wrestler can pursue his sport in a world of one.

It was necessary for Plato to differentiate and clarify the *logos* because he intended to turn it to new and controversial uses. Before him, the pre-Socratic philosophers had used the *logos* to make the material universe intelligible — or as these patriarchs of modern science might have said, "to save the appearances of the external realities." The pre-Socratics had preempted this task from the myth maker who, they felt, did not always account satisfactorily for man's experiences and observations. The myth failed, in their opinion, to furnish man with the modicum of knowledge necessary for him to be able to predict with confidence the outcome of his thoughts and actions. When Hamlet laments, "Our thoughts are ours, their ends none of our own," he expresses the pre-Socratic view of man trapped in a mythological universe without reasoning science.

Plato hoped to advance the *logos* one step farther and use it to save the appearances of the internal realities, man's moral and spiritual nature, the untrammeled wilderness of the *mythos*. The measure of Plato's success in this endeavor will forever be debated, and whether his disciples have managed to press beyond him and claim new tracts of moral and spiritual hinterland for the *logos* remains in doubt. What influences modern education, however, are the reasons proposed for Plato's "failure." These constitute, in short, modern philosophy's attack on language.

Plato's sin (and that of all antiquity) is that he tried to think with language. Language — so the argument goes — is an inept device for reasoning. It is easier for words to grow new meanings than to shed old ones, making language hopelessly conservative. The Oxford English Dictionary credits a little word like *idea* with retaining 12 distinct meanings, dating from Plato to Coleridge (over a hundred years ago). Language is also value-ridden. Few people know *cholesterol* to be a crystalline fatty alcohol, and fewer still know it by its molecular structure, $C_{25}H_{45}OH$, but everyone knows and fears cholesterol's affects on the human body. The purely descriptive scientific term has become a word with repugnant connotations, reducing the value of any food associated with it. Finally, language is often too holistic, protean, and abstract to allow for the precision needed in careful reasoning. Consider the word *valor.* In the *Song of Roland* (Sayers 1973), *valor* describes both Christian and pagan rivals, as well as two men of such contrasting temperaments as Roland and Oliver:

> Roland is fierce and Oliver is wise
> And both for valor may bear away the prize.

The idea of valor, however, remains undivided and untarnished by the logic of events in the narrative. Indeed, that logic suggests valor to be a better guide to action than reason. Had Charlemagne heeded Roland's valorous advice — "Nevermore trust Marsile! Revenge the men this villain made to bleed!" — the tragedy of Roland's defeat through Marsile's treachery would never have come about. The transcendent power of a mere word sways the argument, and unthinking valor turns out to be a better guide to action than Ganelon's reasonable diplomacy.

Words so incurably normative block the progress of the modern era's narrowly operational functions. In the service of science, therefore, modern philosophy attempts to neutralize language, ridding it of values and abstractions, separating it from its fertile source in the mythopoeic imagination, and translating words into counters for playing the elaborate games of a predicate or propositional calculus. Seeing all things in a sort of Heraclitian flux, the modern philosopher shudders at the inadequacy of language to describe this phenomenon. So far as he is concerned, words falsify experience by carrying forward the heretical notion that the underlying old is like the underlying new: *Plus ça change, plus c'est la même chose.* For this reason, he must strip language of its imaginative and suprarational attributes or force upon it a material and descriptive role at odds with its normative and mythopoeic character.

Scientific rationalism and its methods of analysis demand a language of pure denotation to explain programs, techniques, and mechanisms. When the analytical methods and denotative language of scientific rationalism are forced on human learning, however, a reverse distortion occurs, with behaviorism replacing humanism and a mood of professional disinterest supplanting the emotional atmosphere of the ancient classroom. Where distrust of connotative language — with the baggage of value it carries — invades the modern school, there is a methodological tendency to exclude myth and to encourage detached analysis at the expense of the imaginative mind. Words like *valor* fall away, and school becomes a place for learning the function of the *distributor cap.* It makes no more sense, after all, to teach valor by means of a detached analysis than it would to teach the function of a distributor cap through the imaginative mind. A student cannot experience valor through analysis any more than he can a distributor cap through the imagination; hence, the analytical method itself calls into question the utility and reality of such concepts as valor, while affirming that of the distributor cap.

Moreover, by methodologically excluding myth, modern education can no longer pass on the blessings of social cohesiveness and individual coherence. The drift away from connotative language excuses education from urging upon students the moral imperatives inherent in such words as *valor, courage, courtesy, gentleness, honesty,* and *love.* Without the cultural unity provided by myth, the school shrinks from teaching the transcendent meaning and value of human life and settles instead for an analytical pedagogy that often treats human life and art as a programmed mechanism.

III

At the heart of a classical education is the word: the complete mastery of its shades of meaning, of its action-implicit imperatives, of its emotions and values. In ancient times such was the power of the word that it was believed to hold the key to the secrets of the external and internal realities. The word, standing alone, was viewed as a microcosm of both *mythos* and *logos,* making life intelligible. It possessed a mysterious power. God spoke the word, and out of nothing the object came into being. So in the classroom, the simple word *valor* and the fact that the teacher utters it with reverential passion might enliven the student's mind and through the imagination shape his character.

Both myth and reason are built upon the primal word, and both influence the word — myth hoping to enrich its connotative wisdom and reason attempting to sharpen its denotative precision. The word is mastered, in the one instance, through the imagination in an emotional atmosphere and, in the other instance, by means of painstaking analysis in a disinterested mood. Classical education must provide the student with both means of mastering the word, but of preeminent importance to human life and subsequent learning is the cultivation of the imagination. Only through the imagination can virtue be taught and character formed: character that — as Aristotle argues — is the prerequisite for reasoning with true detachment, without purposely or accidentally turning reason into a tool of self-interest.

The preeminence of the connotative word in the marriage of myth and reason is illustrated by the rationalism of the pre-Socratic and the Platonic *logos.* This "new" *logos,* seeking to give a reasonable explanation for man's perplexing observations and experiences of life, shared the same purpose as the *mythos,* but it also anticipated the *mythos* by basing its explanations on direct observation. If there is an inward thought or reason underlying man's experience, the ancient philosopher argued, then it must have existed in the world before the myth embodied it in story form. But the "old" *logos,* the connotative word, already confirms this fact by having supplied myth with the building blocks which, like Chinese ideograms, already embodied and conserved their own inward thoughts and meanings.

One of the most luminous metaphors of all time, Saint John's use of the *logos* to describe Christ, rests on this paradox. Christ, the inward thought or reason, anticipated creation; Christ, the expressor of the inward thought or reason, created; and Christ, the naked aboriginal word itself, became flesh and dwelt among men to become the myth incarnate. Christian faith shares this mystery with language: it is impossible to ascribe a beginning to the word that is not at once denotative and connotative, material and immaterial, temporal and eternal, finite and infinite. Modern philosophy's attack on language as an inept reasoning device begs the question. It may be that man can devise a method of reasoning without language, but the question remains: Would such a reasoning method tell him the truth about himself, or would it force man to label himself incorrectly as a programmed mechanism, so that scientific analysis would remain the preeminent means of studying him?

The modern age's increasing reliance upon scientific rationalism demands that language feed upon appearances rather than upon itself in the mind. When appearance changes, so must language. The positivist logic of modern science shuns the value judgments and aesthetic standards inherent in language, while dismissing the attempt to find mythological verifications and explanations for man's thoughts and observations. The word, no longer a window into the non-existent soul, must describe precisely a palpable reality. It becomes just a counter on life's complicated abacus — that and only that.

Righting this imbalance necessitates a classical understanding of the nature of language, which acknowledges its mystery and weds the word to the mind through the imagination, not exclusively to the external object through the senses. The descriptive weakness of language, for which it is being broken down and rebuilt by the social scientist, is also its prescriptive strength. It clings to the normative essentials underlying the flux of appearances, thereby saving the appearances and making the world intelligible in a way that science cannot. Affirming that precision is a poetic ideal, as well as a requirement of science, teaching that a love of words and an understanding of language is the creative movement of the spirit across the face of the waters, showing how words disclose the transcendent order of meaning and value behind the curtain of a transient world — these beloved and arduous tasks of the classical school-master abide.

3

TEACHING THE FATHER OF THE MAN

Rigorous teachers seized my youth,
And purged its faith and trimmed its fire,
Showed me the high, white star of Truth,
There bade me gaze and there aspire.

—*Matthew Arnold*

I

Forgetting the notorious Sophists, let us imagine that there exists a difference between the itinerant teacher of the Roman and early Christian eras, who became caught up in the imperial craving after profit and power, and the master of earlier times, who usually managed to practice his gentle art without succumbing to the enticements of gain and glory. Let us examine this admittedly idealized version of the ancient schoolmaster in the hope that he will teach us something about what the aims and methods of the teacher ought to be. To begin with, he possesses two outstanding traits. First, his temper and behavior are governed by ideas: his life maintains that perfect balance between thought and action, theory and practice that makes him seem to his students the very incarnation of his lessons. Second, he has a broad and penetrating curiosity and a delightfully dialectical mind, eager to devise and test a hypothesis, quick to challenge ideas and observations, but slow to accept an *aitia* (a first or final cause, an incontrovertible ground), even though, like Democritus, he would rather discover an *aitia* than be king of the Persians. A habit of provoking and asking questions of no immediate practical value accompanies this friendly, dialectical disposition. Of course, our idealized teacher is Socrates.

Socrates was a nuisance to many of the educators of his day, the utilitarian Sophists who were experts at teaching their students how to function within the madding city of Athens. A Sophist tended to accept the "givens": an advocacy system that had lost the understanding of justice, a mob opinion no longer sensitive to the demands of truth and beauty. He taught his students simply how to do what had to be done to get along: how, when necessary, to make the weaker argument appear the stronger. The Sophist lived and taught in a world of appearances, accepting these appearances (about which hung the aura of permanence and palpability) as dogma, as "givens," as reality. His first principle was: Do not question the appearances; there is no practical value in doing so.

Then along came Socrates, questioning the world of appearances, a world the Sophist thought he had mastered, a world from which the Sophist won his daily bread. "How if it feeds us," the Sophist asked, "can it be bad or illusory?" Yet the world of appearances is always crumbling down, and the Sophist, for personal short-term gain, unwittingly hastens its demise by teaching his selfish and ruthless students the frailities of the system. The utilitarian educator, then as now, is a sort of intellectual fifth column. He ridicules the impalpable, idealistic aims of the Socratic teacher, who threatens him by questioning not only his methods and results, but his sacred premises. Without the Socratic teacher, however, there is no saving the appearances, and the appearances, however lovely or useful, are doomed — as is the civilization whose unsaved appearances become its idols, empty of meaning, empty of faith, empty of transcendent value.

II

There is another idealized version of the ancient schoolmaster, less dependent than the Socratic one upon the idiosyncratic genius of the individual teacher. Like Socrates, this fellow seems to his students to embody his lessons, but his aims and methods are ostensibly more practical and positive, less philosophical than Socrates'. Whereas Socrates challenges the appearances, he uses a great tradition of learning in the arts, letters, and sciences to excite in his students a vision of those enduring values and truths that underlie the world of appearances. Once armed with the wisdom of this tradition, he believes, his students will understand justice, heed the demands of truth and beauty, and lead the life of virtue — no matter how alluring all appearances to the contrary. This teacher's name is Isokrates.

Isokrates finds his modern antagonist not so much in the utilitarian Sophist as in what we might call the *romantic school of child psychology.* This is the school that despite *The Turn of the Screw, Lord of the Flies,* and *High Wind in Jamaica* believes in the ideal child. The seventh-grade teacher of this school presides over a classroom where 12-year-old values hold sway. The defender of the romantic school argues that childhood ought to be a time of enjoyment, pleasure, and freedom. Sometimes Piaget is dragged in by the heels to show why children cannot learn or suffer academic discipline. Let us not, pleads the romantic, force a child into the drudgery of scholarship before he has outlived his playful, innocent youth. This argument, however, turns on a false view of scholarship, as well as on a naive interpretation of child psychology. Perhaps those who believe it concern themselves with an ideal of how children ought to behave because they have no vision of what their students ought to be as adults.

In any case, Isokrates' educative aim was to form an adult, not to develop a child, and his method was to teach the knowledge of a mature mind, not to offer relevant learning experiences at the level of his student's stage of psychological development. His methods surely had their shortcomings, but on their behalf, it might be said that logical progression is more readily ascertained and agreed upon than psychological order. Moreover, where the two are not coterminous, what may be proper psychological order may also be logical chaos. It is the challenge of teaching to understand what form advanced concepts ought to take at a rudimentary level of psychological development, while it is the challenge of learning to discipline the unruly and discursive mind, adjusting its disorderliness through rigorous study to the order of logical processes found outside it in the subject matter.

Although his aims and methods accounted for an almost complete indifference to child psychology, Isokrates must have perceived childhood as a period of becoming rather than as a state of being. Children, he recognized, want to be brought up; they do not want to remain 12-year-olds. The healthy child wants to *become* an adult, just as the mature adult wants to *be* an adult. For this reason, Isokrates taught his students what in fact they wanted to know: how to think and act like a mature person. This, of course, is not equivalent to being a mature person, but it points out the essentially imitative nature of the rhetorician's educational method and explains his compulsion to be an exemplary model of his lessons. It also helps account for the extraordinarily high standards of achievement he expected of his young pupils, demanding of them an unusual command of language and knowledge of myth, always believing that the mastery of these subjects would shape in them a mature and sensitive style and conscience.

Isokrates, like Aristotle, looked upon childhood as the crucial period for forming the life of virtue in a person. To set childhood aside as a time of enjoyment, pleasure, and freedom would not only cripple the child's chances for future learning, but would condemn him to the exasperating, enervating, and illusory life of pleasure. Isokrates' avoidance of this romantic fallacy suggests, paradoxically, that he regarded education with the mind of a child. Of towering importance to the child are not the playful, innocent moments remembered by the adult who nears death, but the hard-won progress he makes as a child toward his image of adulthood. He measures his greatest achievements and most agonizing defeats against this image. When his teacher holds out to him only an image of how 12-year-olds ought to think and act, his hope of growth wavers, and he becomes restive and inattentive.

Isokrates had little in common with the modern teacher who fantasizes an ideal child and bases his child-centered learning on the nostalgic writings of Rousseau. Where Isokrates made demands of the child, the modern teacher seeks to make concessions. Where Isokrates held out to the child a bright, lofty image of adulthood, the modern teacher suspects ideal images of being arbitrary, superficial nuisances (as well as anxiety producing). Where Isokrates sought to form a virtuous man, the modern teacher asks with casual guile — What is virtue? — expecting an answer no more than jesting Pilate. At root, not science but skepticism flavors his theoretical gruel. *Child-centered learning* is a high-sounding euphemism for his refusal to admit a connection between what makes a person virtuous and what constitutes an educated person. Consequently, his child-centered education produces the exact opposite of an educated person: a self-centered adult.

III

Our idealized schoolmasters of antiquity never doubted, although they seldom agreed upon, the connection between the virtuous and the educated man. If alive today and asked — What is virtue? — they would probably confess to her owning a diverse wardrobe. They might even refer us to Bertrand Russell's (1973) description of the historical changes in virtue's apparel:

> Dr. Arnold wanted "humbleness of mind," a quality not possessed by Aristotle's "magnanimous man." Nietzsche's ideal is not that of Christianity. No more is Kant's: for while Christ enjoins love, Kant teaches that no action of which love is the motive can be truly virtuous. And even people who agree as to the ingredients of a good character may differ as to their relative importance. One man will emphasize courage, another learning, another kindliness, and another rectitude. One man, like the elder Brutus, will put duty to the State above family affection; another, like Confucius, will put family affection first. *All these divergences will produce differences as to education. We must have some concept of the kind of person we wish to produce, before we can have any definite opinion as to the education which we consider best* [Italics mine].

But the fact that virtue may be dressed up in many ways did not make her less real to the ancients — or the life of virtue less useful to them as a beacon guiding the best education.

In his quest for the best education, the ancient schoolmaster possessed two advantages over the modern educator. First, he knew exactly what kind of a person he wished to produce. He shared with his contemporaries a prescriptive understanding of man inherited from the past and embodied in the Ideal Type of the *mythos*. This lent considerable agreement in substance when it came time to tick off the items on the list of what every educated man ought to know. Second, he agreed in form upon an inquiry-based or knowledge-centered — as opposed to a child-centered — approach to education. Whether he was a philosopher hoping to elicit knowledge or a rhetorician hoping to implant it, he ignored the "child" and appealed directly to the "father of the man" within his student.

This knowledge-centered approach led many schoolmasters to assign the most difficult studies first, with the expectation that having mastered these, their students would have no trouble with whatever followed. Put thus abstractly and unconditionally, the classical approach sounds harsh indeed — and I would be inclined to doubt its efficacy were it not for the piano lessons of my boyhood days. There lived in the neighborhood where I grew up two elderly ladies, piano teachers, whose divergent methods of instruction seemed inconsequential at the time. At the unripe ages of six and seven, my best friend and I were placed under their respective tutelage.

My friend began, as I recall, with a simple minuet by Mozart, which he was expected to commit to memory — a monstrously formidable and uncongenial first assignment, we both agreed. My obliging teacher, on the other hand, assigned me a one-note "samba" from an illustrated book of graded exercises. Four years later, I concluded my graded exercises with a banal rendition of something entitled "The Lone Ranger" from Barber's overworked *Overture*. Along the way, I had learned to play a tune by rolling an orange over the black keys. While I was losing interest in graded exercises, however, my friend — after a month of agonizing over Mozart before breakfast and after school — went on to play with elegance and precision the Brahms, Chopin, and Liszt that my illiterate fingers will never coax out of a keyboard.

Clearly, one cannot generalize on the basis of one experience: had I begun with a Mozart minuet, my appreciation for music might have died at the age of seven. But the knowledge-centered approach to education recalls to the sophisticated modern mind what the ancients understood as the virtues of adversity. What a child can do should not become the sole judge of what the student is asked to do. "A pupil from whom nothing is ever demanded which he cannot do, never does all he can," wrote John Stuart Mill (1944). The activity of learning takes place in a no-man's land between what the student can accomplish and what he may not be able to accomplish. This fact sets up a creative tension in education, to which both student and teacher must become accustomed and responsive. The teacher who refrains from assigning *Silas Marner* to his 12-year-old students because George Eliot's syntax is too complicated and her periodic sentences too long may be avoiding this creative tension. If so, he should not be a teacher. His students may never know the joy of reading George Eliot because he shirks a calling in which the daily work is accomplished through the virtues of adversity.

IV

The modern reader will be surprised to learn that classical education's emphasis on mastering an inherited body of knowledge rather than on developing a happy, well-adjusted child makes possible a profound and intimate relationship between the schoolmaster and his pupils. Knowledge — the activity of learning — gives teacher and student a common ground for friendship, while accentuating their unequal status. Students become the disciples of their teacher, so to speak, forming around him what in ancient times was referred to poetically as a *chorus,* or a *thiasos* ("fraternity"). Teachers then exercised such a profound influence over their students that the charge against Socrates of corrupting youth was not at all an uncommon one.

Socrates himself identified this strong spiritual bond between the master and his pupils as *eros,* the source of virtue in learning. Today, *eros* simply means romantic love, but to the ancients it involved a much richer concept, joining the mind of the student with the mind of his master, uniting the idea and the deed. *Eros* charged the air of the ancient classroom with the genuine feeling of the master for his subject and for his pupils: the emotional commitment necessary for capturing the imagination of his students. One can neither know what virtue is nor benefit from the knowledge of it, the ancients believed, unless one participated theoretically and practically in virtue, unless one abandoned oneself — as in love — to act in accordance with the good and the beautiful, in headlong pursuit of excellence and moderation. "The great secret of morals is love," wrote Shelley (Baker 1951) in his *Defense of Poetry,*

> or a going out of our own nature, and an identification of ourselves with the beautiful which exists in thought, action, or person, not our own. A man, to be greatly good, must imagine intensely and comprehensively; he must put himself in the place of another and of many others; the pains and pleasures of his species must become his own.

But in an age such as ours, unable to distinguish between the erotic and the pornographic, between the love that moves the spheres and enlightens men's minds and a love kindled in the loins, this concept is incomprehensible.

The ancients preferred oral teaching over the impersonal study of the written word. Talk was freer, more intimate, and depended on the teacher's lively intelligence and superior knowledge to keep it orbiting around essential concerns. The teacher risked himself: he stood for something. He had not only examined all sides of the question; he had chosen one, defended it, and expected his students to do likewise. Because he professed to teach the knowledge that makes a man virtuous and wise, his life had to illuminate his teachings.

Ideally, the ancient schoolmaster's teaching obliterated the modern distinction between scholarship and instruction. His logical, probing, imaginative discourse was a kind of ongoing research into the internal and external realities. Unlike the lonely drudgery of modern scholarship, with its guarded opinions and pettifogging zeal, classical scholarship inhabits the classroom and the open air, the drinking parties and the playing fields. It is a social and, sometimes, a festive event — witty, graceful, spontaneous, yet inexorably logical when it wishes to be, pressing a point far beyond where the writer dares go in print. Most importantly, classical scholarship's fundamentally human, normative concerns touch the lives of people, whatever their professions and predilections, and prepares them to live more fully and worthily in all their domains — the individual, the social, and the religious.

Classical education challenges both teacher and pupil: the one to justify his superior wisdom and intellectual skill; the other to win his teacher's praise by matching his performance. The personal element in their learning compensates for the lack of educational psychology, teaching aids, and learning paraphernalia. The pupil becomes a part of his teacher's own studies, his intimate relationship with the schoolteacher making him, perforce, even more than an observer — an assistant and participant in the ongoing inquiry. A lively dialectic arises, educating both. In truth, such mutual learning is the unavoidable, happy consequence of a profound and intimate relationship between the teacher and his pupil.

Yet with a weird logic, today's professional educator argues that mutual learning implies equal ignorance. He substitutes class preparation and teaching technique for knowledge and *eros*. He measures the personal element in education according to the teacher's understanding of the student mind, not vice versa. He rejects the classical view that a thorough inquiry not only into "one's field" but into its far-flung relations is the best preparation for teaching. He demands that the modern teacher, like himself, become a student of education: inquiring into the nature of the immature mind and mastering the techniques for accommodating it and for making the school's graded exercises and relevant learning experiences tolerable. Although this arrangement nicely guarantees full enrollments for the schools of education, it exhausts the teacher's patience and does nothing to meet the teacher's need for real knowledge.

In many instances, the modern lesson plan disguises the teacher's embarrassing lack of knowledge, especially of the sort relating that day's gobbets of information or activity to fundamental human concerns. The ideas and beliefs men live for and die with seldom come out of lesson plans, but the lesson plan satisfies the teacher's need for an appearance of knowledge. To foster this appearance, new courses and new departments spring up in the hope that once pulverized, the body of knowledge will yield up all its secrets in one of its stray particles even to the most indolent mind. If that fails (and no one doubts that it will), we shall at least satisfy the conditions of erudition by having mastered a single particle of knowledge: the sacred academic discipline. At least, that is, until Socrates returns from the dead and asks what our discrete, trifling particles of knowledge have to do with the whole of it, yes, and with whatever it is that makes a man virtuous and wise.

4

THE TYRANNIZING IMAGE

I think continually of those who were truly great.
Who, from the womb, remembered the soul's history
Through corridors of light where the hours are suns,
Endless and singing. Whose lovely ambition
Was that their lips, still touched with fire,
Should tell of the spirit clothed from head to foot in
* song.*
And who hoarded from the spring branches
The desires falling across their bodies like blossoms.

What is precious is never to forget . . .

—Stephen Spender

I

An Ideal Type tyrannized classical education. The ancient schoolmaster in his intense struggle to achieve a living synthesis of thought and action exemplified this Ideal and passed it on to his pupils by inviting them to share in his struggle for self-knowledge and self-mastery, the immature mind participating in the mature. Against this Ideal were the master's achievements and his pupils' judged. All fell short, of course, but some — and here's the rub — far less short than others. Although the Ideal Type no longer receives attention from the educational theorist, it still is used in contemporary judgment of both teachers and students. Whether in Thomas Merton's reverent portrait of Mark Van Doren or in Edmund Wilson's urbane acclaim of Christian Gauss, it is apparent that the greatest teachers still exhibit an Ideal in their speech and behavior and in their normative approach to learning. Their lessons spring to life in the moral climate surrounding them.

Defining this Ideal Type resembles the attempt to define a term like *liberalism*. Like two irresistible magnets, liberalism and the Ideal Type encase themselves in an almost impenetrable mass of diverse opinion. In his search for definitions, the student is liable to mistake an affixed fragment for the magnet itself and, consequently, to define the liberalism of William Gladstone or Franklin Roosevelt exclusive of John Stuart Mill or Bertrand Russell. After surveying the chaos, he may throw up his hands in disgust, protesting that only a concept so abstract and general as to be meaningless could attract such a diversity of people and opinion. But if the student wishes to explain the past and make sense of the present, he must persevere in his search and discover the meaning of liberalism.

Both liberalism and the Ideal Type can only be defined by studying their manifestations; the modern method of collecting samples of liberalism and the ancient manner of gathering examples of the Ideal Type illustrate the difference between these two concepts. Liberalism is an aposterioric accident of history, describing at different times and in different places a religious movement, a theory of economics, and a political philosophy. The modern student of liberalism examines the writers and actors in this relatively modern historical drama and develops a series of descriptive hypotheses that change as the appearances of liberalism change. Thus described by an evolving sequence of experiential hypotheses, liberalism soon loses its original form. The hypothesis of a hundred years ago is unrecognizable today; only the word *liberalism* remains. Some writers even trot out the century-old hypothesis as their modern definition of conservatism.

Classical education's Ideal Type, on the contrary, anticipates history. Time may age it, softening its Homeric edges, but neither time nor place can alter its identity. It is an aprioric necessity of human existence, a concomitant of human life, prescribing for all time the standard by which men shall judge themselves and others. Whereas man can exist alone or in the company of his fellows without liberal religion, liberal economics, and liberal politics, he cannot escape the tyranny of the Ideal Type. In this regard, the *Ideal* shares the paradox of the *Word*: it is impossible to ascribe a beginning to it that is not at once denotative and connotative, material and immaterial, temporal and eternal, finite and infinite.

The Ideal Type, like the Word, unites the warring *mythos* and *logos*. Poetry and philosophy both seek to explain the condition of human life through some formal idealization of experience that in identifying the material universe's immanent order as allegorical, logical, or arithmetical, prescribes as it describes. Myth began this process by defining the Ideal Type in the works and days of men. The myth maker observed or imagined an action that he and his fellows inherently admired. He recorded it, and the universal appeal of the Ideal emanating from his record constituted mankind's best proof of an aprioric moral absolute. Later, *reason* measured the Ideal — the tyrannizing image of human perfection — as the distance between what man is and what he ought to be. From the Proverbs of Solomon to the Golden Sayings of Epictetus, philosophy tried to generalize upon the myth maker's particulars in order to establish a table of virtues or a code of conduct in accordance with the Ideal Type. In this way, the philosopher hoped to turn poetry to practical use and help man span the gap between what he is and what he ought to be.

The ancient student of the Ideal Type, therefore, started out with the dogma of a moral ideal called *kalokagathia* — a man both beautiful and good. When he asked — What is excellence in man? — he did not so much seek his answer in poetry and philosophy as he sought illustration and confirmation of his answer there. The answer, as it were, preceded the question and the questioner, but both were needed to elicit it. Each new generation of students began at the beginning with Homer and Hesiod, refining, perhaps reinterpreting, the primal stamp, but never presuming to set up a rival ideal and never daring to give in entirely to pragmatic doubts. Any rival ideal would have met with sheer incomprehension, as Saint Paul discovered on Mars Hill, and a worse fate awaited the doubter, as the Athenians learned when their Syracusan debacle (according to Thucydides) followed hard on their ruthless realpolitik at Melos. Because it was rooted in the dogma of a prescriptive view of man, the Ideal withstood the ravages of time and change. Like the life of virtue at its heart, it remained immediately recognizable in all ages and to all men, whether it wore the mail armor of a Christian Richard or the flowing robes of a Moslem Saladin.

II

A composite image of imperatives for human behavior, the Ideal Type is a central concern of classical education, but teaching it presents two problems. First, owing to its aprioric and therefore dogmatic nature, its lesson threatens to be boring. What could be more stultifying than having to memorize page after page of aphoristic wisdom and having to listen hour after hour to a teacher's windy commentary? But here the myth maker comes to the rescue. The poet, Plato (Jowett 1969) writes in the *Phaedra*, "clothes all the great deeds accomplished by the men of old with glory, and thus educates those who come after." The poet's myth teaches the Ideal Type by example, not by precept, and allows the student through his imagination to participate in the past, partaking of the Ideal. Often the student is asked — paraphrasing Shelley — to go out of his own nature: to imagine himself in the sandals of some mythical or historical figure. How would you have advised the Senate, his teacher might ask him, had you been Regulus returned from Carthage with the ultimatum?

In ancient times, the poet's penchant for personifying the Ideal Type spread to other writers, including the historians, who were not above occasionally assisting the Ideal in judging their narrative's characters. "What follows merits the attention of those who despise all human qualities in comparison with riches, and think there is no room for great honors or for worth but amidst a profusion of wealth," Livy (1922) paused in his account of Cincinnatus to point out. He then goes on to present a familiar Roman self-portrait: the good, simple, humble man "intent upon some rustic task" in a small republic of cabbage-eating farmers absent-mindedly conquering the world. Livy wants not only to inform, but to teach his reader by example the style of life he believes to be most consistent with the Ideal Type; and not only is his method of teaching the Ideal more exciting, but his examples strike nearer the truth of the Ideal than any aphorisms or proverbs could. "In all discussions of actions," states Aristotle (1974) in his lecture on *Ethics*, "general statements cover a larger number of cases, but particular ones come nearer to the truth of the matter. The sphere of action is particulars, so our statements must be shown to be in harmony with the particular application of them."

As Aristotle's observation suggests, the second problem with teaching the Ideal Type is that it falls into the sphere of action. The lesson of the Ideal is not an item of information or a series of descriptive hypotheses whose validity depends on scholarly detachment. The Ideal demands action, and the lesson must therefore be taught in accordance with the dynamic, imperative nature of the subject. The use of inspiring or repugnant examples in some measure accomplishes this purpose; but the ancients knew that man cannot comprehend the whole dogma and live according to it simply by memorizing its general precepts or by imitating its particular examples. Man must also challenge its parts.

Now, this challenge composes the dynamic, dialectical means of teaching dogma: the conscious process of negating parts of the Ideal at various levels of human activity in order to prove these parts and their relation to the whole. The teacher may ask, for example: What would human life be like without an ideal or moral category of courage? Could man survive without courage or ascribe meaning to his actions without it? Can we fully explain human life without taking an ideal of courage into account? The dialectical challenge to courage comes to most men, sooner or later, in the form of a pusillanimous act. For the man who fails this challenge, his action — however regrettable — deepens his understanding of what courage is and of why it is fundamental to human life.

Classical education, however, does not encourage students to carry out willful acts of cowardice in order to learn courage. Rather, the school seeks to habituate young people to act in accordance with all parts of the Ideal Type, and in so doing, it hopes to spare them the pain and possible danger of cowardly behavior by presenting the dialectical negations within the tradition of arts, letters, and sciences under study. By reading the poet Archilochus (Trypanis 1971), for example, the student vicariously negates the superficial notion of courage sometimes associated with the old heroic ideal.

> I do not like a tall general, nor a long-shanked one, nor one who is proud of his hair, nor one who is partly shaved. Give me one who is short and bandy-legged to look at, but who walks firmly and is full of courage.

Archilochus' ridicule of the heroic stereotype of a military leader clarifies the truth of the Ideal: that true generalship is a matter of courage, not of bearing. Ancient literature thrives on this sort of dialectical attack on nonessential characteristics attaching themselves to the Ideal.

Likewise in the classical school, students are often asked to play the "devil's advocate," defending Cleon's demagoguery or Alcibiades' treachery. This exercise not merely sharpens a student's rhetorical wits, but it negates certain parts of the Ideal in such a way that the negation demonstrates the nonessential nature of these parts. One probably learns more about what is essential to the Ideal Type when trying to defend Alcibiades and the consequences of his treachery than when excoriating him. In any case, classical education eventually fills the young person's head with the sound of voices: the impassioned debate of the many great figures of myth and history concerning what is good, beautiful, and excellent in man. Through his imagination, the student participates in this dialectical confabulation, and his thoughts and actions become literally involved with the Ideal Type. The Ideal is refined, and action and thought join inextricably in the life of virtue.

What is implied and demanded by the Ideal Type as manifest in the *mythos* and the *logos*? This is a central concern of classical instruction. All study, all thought, all creativity draws its significance from this moral preoccupation. To produce a man or woman whose life conforms to the Ideal in every detail is education's supremely moral aim. The Ideal extends to each student a personal imperative and hope, motivating him to excel in his studies. It lays claim to the student's will, capitalizing early on the student's youthful desire to grow up to be a Regulus or a Cincinnatus, a Jefferson or a Lincoln; and it promises him a wealth of inner resources independent of outward circumstance, like those the cabbage-eating farmers of the early Roman and American republics possessed. The consummation of this imperative and this hope is the harmonious balance found in Aristotle's life of virtue.

III

What accounts, then, for the sad fate of the Ideal Type in the modern era? Why do the educational theorists pay it no mind? A statement made at the conclusion of James McLachlan's recent study of *American Boarding Schools* captures, in what reads like a cliché, something of the current attitude concerning ideals: "As a society changes, its ideal types change. With such shifts the aims and methods of education also change." But, is this right? Should ideal types, like cosmetic fashions, constantly be changing? These questions underline the problem with McLachlan's typical nonnormative presentation of his well-researched package of information: it does not stir a response in the reader; it fails to judge issues that cry out for judgment; it dresses up colorful moral dilemmas in drab amoral prose (so as not to forfeit a claim to objectivity). Thus we see the falsifying influence of the social sciences upon the study of man, the deception that inevitably arises when nonnormative methods are applied to the study of normative subject matter. Is it worth the appearance of objectivity to deceive the reader in this way? I think not. The irony of this deception is heightened, however, when it attends the conclusion of a historical study about one of the last American institutions to articulate the Ideal Type. Nevertheless, it helps to dramatize the overwhelming victory of relativism and scientific realism in modern educational theory.

Relativism flourishes in a setting where appearances become tantamount to reality and where there is no longer any transcendent basis for judging one appearance as better than another. In an age of appearances, the ideal becomes relative to changes in fashion, opinion, and taste — the Edwardian hero succeeds the Victorian hero, the hero of Horatio Alger grows overnight into a playboy. At one moment, the ideal may favor charm, at another efficiency, but in any case, it is an essentially superficial ideal, a momentary phenomenon. Most educators today have the good sense to distrust such fleeting ideals, pointing out their lack of substance and enduring value. Yet at the same time, these educators, skeptical of any reality beyond the appearances, dismiss as "problematic" the entire question of teaching an Ideal Type or of teaching in prescribed moral categories. They end up educating in a void — distrusting the appearances and disbelieving the immanent reality.

This state of affairs has a long history. The Ideal Type began to decline as soon as it emerged badly bruised from the Low Middle Ages. For religious reasons, it had already lost much of its dialectical vitality. By formalizing the Ideal within ecclesiastical dogma, the Church at Rome and the schoolmen in Paris reduced the Ideal to a ritual and a creed, while refusing to permit the laity to challenge its parts in the life of faith. On a practical level, the teaching of the Ideal by example suffered for lack of a reliable high-quality *mythos*. The rich, ancient *mythos* of Greece and Rome was lost or bowdlerized, and the simple Christian *mythos* had been plastered over with popular, irrelevant, and usually outlandish legends of the saints. But even against these long odds, the Ideal survived in the person of Chaucer's "parfait, gentil knyght."

Just when Renaissance and Church reform promised to restore much of the ancient *mythos* and *logos* and to chisel away the cheap plaster that encased the central figure of the Christian *mythos*, the state began having pragmatic doubts about the efficacy of the Ideal Type. The crowned heads of Europe did not wish to share their thrones with a tyrannizing image any more than with the pope and his nuncios. The fate of Thomas More, the great exemplar of the Ideal Type in his day, symbolizes the effect of these doubts. Henry VIII wanted there to be only one tyrant in More's life, but instead, he saw three: a Church, an Ideal, and himself. Not wishing to rule his subjects as part of a triumvirate, the king had More's head chopped off and — condescending to play the part of Christ — made the Church another one of his brides.

In political exile, its dialectic dead, the Ideal Type no longer commanded the wide respect or generated the great enthusiasm it once had. By the eighteenth century, the final phase of the war on the tyrannizing image was well under way. In certain respects, this phase resembled the early American Indian wars — one side armed with musketry, the other with only bows and arrows. The musketry of the Ideal's opponents was the skepticism of scientific realism, expressed in Bacon's marvelously dismissive phrase: "since I cannot be called on to abide by the sentence of a tribunal which is itself on trial." The skepticism of scientific realism is only assuaged by empirical, palpable, cash-value proofs; it is not impressed by the logical arguments and mythological evidences of an Ideal Type. In yet other respects, this final phase of the Ideal's demise resembled the Napoleonic wars, with conscription universal and muskets handed out to everyone. It takes little training to doubt what lies beyond the five senses and no effort at all to drop the stern demands of noblesse oblige.

The war itself developed along two broad fronts: the one popular and political; the other, philosophical. On the popular, political front, the elitist and tyrannizing influences of the Ideal Type came under attack. "Whence came this Ideal, anyway? What makes its claim legitimate? Why should all men be obliged to fall under the influence of a single Ideal?" sniped the rhetorical sharp-shooters at the Ideal's exposed flanks. Meanwhile, reinforcements from the battle-hardened armies of the great bourgeois revolutions began pouring in. Rousseau at their head identified the Ideal with *l'ancien régime* — said it smelled of parasols and periwigs, of the anacronistic notion that all men, noble savages by nature good, are not born equal. After all, if man is by birth and instinct already good and democratically equal, his own personal ideal is surely as good as any other's. What need has he of correction, to say nothing of conversion? Let education release his inviolable personal ideal and not impose the arbitrary and stultifying restraints of an extrinsic tyrannizing image. Leave the no longer prescriptive matters of conscience and style up to the individual, and leave the individual free to develop these as he sees fit and is able, without the threat of censure or of failure. There is no need for him to appeal from his own to any authority outside himself.

Descartes led the philosophical attack on the Ideal Type. At first, his assault seemed modest and deceptively tangential to the work of education. He argued that education ought to concern itself only with ideas that are precise and certain beyond any possibility of doubt. What benefit is there in teaching what after close scrutiny may prove false? Difficulties arise, however, when one begins to doubt everything in the hope of finding an indubitable truth. What is to be the test for indubitable truth, anyway? Three hundred years ago, the answer to this question had almost nothing to do with science as we know it today. The dogmas of religion and historical wisdom were still potent forces, necessary for making truths legitimate, and the princely aim of philosophy was still, strictly speaking, metaphysical — a reasonable search after transcendent values, an inquiry into how men should live their lives. The Ideal Type combined the insights of religion, history, and philosophy and stood — although precari-ously — in its impalpable glory at the center of learning as the supreme test for truth.

But Descartes, having swept away these insights with his famous skepticism, demanded a new and more humble beginning for knowledge. It was only natural that science would afford this fresh start. Although narrowly confined to the material universe, the methods of science promised a considerable degree of precise and certain knowledge. Scientific knowledge, however, was objective and universal in a way that seemed to invalidate these claims on the part of the Ideal Type. Whereas the objectivity of science does not depend upon the observer, the Ideal Type possesses no objective reality outside the life of the person manifesting it. Whereas the truths of science are universal because any man who follows the right methods can arrive at them, the truths of the Ideal Type result from insights that can be encouraged through an imitation of language and myth, but not taught as a method or recipe.

For reasons to be considered in the next chapter, the scientific understanding of objectivity and universality gradually replaced the classical one. The Ideal Type, unable to justify itself in terms of science and therefore at a loss to prove itself "real," faded from the classroom. The laboratory took its place. A strict analysis conquered the classroom and expelled the normative study of arts and letters, which had for centuries contributed dialectically to the Ideal. One no longer heard questions reminiscent of Plutarch raised in the classroom: "Tell me Johnny, how did Jefferson think a good man ought to live his life?" Insight fell under the methodological axe, and research began to satisfy the demands for thought. Education entered a new era of the real.

IV

The education of the real prepares a student for an efficient existence. It supplies him with a knowledge of precise and certain ideas (facts) and presents him with whatever repetitive and highly functional technique (programs) will assure his success. Success in the realm of the real tends to be measured against selfish and tangible standards: money, power, and pleasure. No longer does education thwart man's lowest desires, or fire his best dreams, or condemn society's perennial allurements by holding up a tyrannizing image of what man ought to be. We have avoided the tough old question — How can an inquiring mind be freely developed under the rule of a tyrannizing image? — simply by ignoring the Ideal. But now, we face a new and even tougher question — What is the value of our knowledge if it is not in some way connected to the Ideal? Is not scientific knowledge ultimately dehumanizing, pointless, and destructive — inhibiting our sense of responsibility, while heightening our powers — if not balanced against a knowledge of what is good and an ideal of how man ought to live? "Hence the strange combination of a sense of power and a sense of insecurity which has taken up its abode in the soul of modern man," writes Ortega y Gasset (1975).

Another way of making this distinction between the education of the Ideal and the education of the real is by comparing the ancient and modern means or norms. The Greek doctrine of the Golden Mean prescribed man as he ought to be — physically poised, mentally balanced and rounded off, thoughtful in action and active in thought: the living embodiment of the Ideal Type. The modern mean, on the other hand, defines the individual as he is in relation to a statistical point. The Golden Mean was a dynamic principle; the modern mean is a static one. Ancient man strove to fulfill in his person the Golden Mean and was rewarded with rare moments of fleeting achievement; modern man, however, is always at — or so many points off — the modern mean.

Education's graduation from a Golden Mean philosophy to one of statistical mean is not yet complete. Despite our failure nowadays to agree on a Golden Mean, the demands of the Ideal Type persistently tug at our hearts. These we dismiss as subjective longings for some bygone era. We quiet these urges by reminding ourselves of how psychologically damaging and undemocratic a Golden Mean philosophy is to the student who must endure the tensions of constant self-denial and self-control in pursuit of the Ideal. Besides, it adds enormously to the burden of being a teacher, who must struggle to embody the Ideal and who must take responsibility for cultivating in his students a sense of conscience and style both inside and outside of the classroom. How much easier and safer it is to adopt the philosophy of the modern mean. Judging the student against what he is or against what his peers are, after dividing them by their number, seems far less arbitrary and demanding. What could be more democratic and less controversial? How could a student fail to measure up to what he is? Unfortunately, however, the statistical mean is a solution with mathematical — but not human — efficacy.

The past instructs us that man has only understood himself and mastered himself in pursuit of a self-transcendent Ideal, a Golden Fleece, a Promised Land, a Holy Grail, a numinous windmill. He defines himself in the quest, not on Kalypso's unblown isle, where he is only judged against himself, where all obstacles are removed, where the question of human significance seems insignificant, and where there are no moral restraints or binding ideals. On Kalypso's idyllic estate, Odyssean man is a nobody. He languishes in egocentric frustration, self-doubt, and insecurity. In many ways, he is a portrait of the modern student, seated "on the vacant beach with a shattered heart, scanning the sea's bare horizon with wet eyes" (Fitzgerald 1963). Only Odysseus' knowledge of the past — his longing for Ithaka, Penelope, and Telemakhos — keeps him alive; and only the responsibility he takes for that knowledge rescues him from Kalypso's pointless life of pleasure.

5

SAVING THE APPEARANCES

He also said to the multitudes, "When you see a cloud rising in the west, you say at once, 'A shower is coming'; and so it happens. And when you see the south wind blowing, you say, 'There will be scorching heat'; and it happens. You hypocrites! You know how to interpret the appearances of earth and sky; but why do you not know how to interpret the present time? And why do you not judge for yourselves what is right?"

—Saint Luke, the physician

I

Science is not an ancient category. The Greek words describing what we today think of as science — *peri physeos historia* ("inquiry concerning nature"), *philosophia* ("philosophy"), *theoria* ("speculation"), and *episteme* ("knowledge") — indicate the extent to which philosophy dominated scientific investigation. Although the ancients possessed a scientific method of sorts and such scientific instruments as the dioptra and the astrolabe, they are often criticized for failing to set up controlled experiments and for not observing nature closely and critically. Hipparchus' work in observational astronomy, Archimedes' experiments in mechanics, and Herophilus' scrupulous human dissections might argue with this criticism, but they do not belie the ancients' preference for abstract thought over empirical research. Their reasons for distrusting empirical research all stemmed from philosophy. First, the apparent irregularity and instability of nature, not the inadequacy of their methods or instruments, led the ancients to question the reliability of experiment and observation, especially as methods of proof. Second, having recently acquired a compelling system of logic, they preferred to concentrate on abstract, deductive methods of proof (synthesis) rather than on concrete, inductive methods of discovery (analysis).

Finally, they looked upon the natural world as a representation of an impalpable, unchanging reality full of meaning and truth — not as something existing in its own right apart from either the will of God or the vagaries of human perception.

We observe these reasons at work in Plato's influential theory of knowledge. Plato taught that knowledge exists on three levels, the lowest and crudest of these being simple observation. Since the observable world is constantly in a state of flux, no fixed knowledge of it can be had. One can only attain fixed knowledge at the highest level of knowledge by escaping the fickle world of sense perception and by contemplating the divine Reality, the *aitia*, the Supreme Good underlying it. In between these two extremes lies what Plato considered a "bastard" form of knowledge created by the union of sense knowledge's concreteness and divine knowledge's abstractness. Plato cautioned his students against expecting to find true knowledge at this intermediate level, but he recommended its study as a good preparation for moving on to the contemplative level.

The student of intermediate knowledge might attempt to explain his crude observations of the movement of the planets by hypothesizing some underlying geometric design, but he never expected concrete and exact results from his investigations. He was too concerned with the logical derivation of his conclusions to worry about their empirical verifiability. He was not, for instance, particularly offended by Aristarchus' heliocentric theory; but like those who centuries later refused to look through Galileo's telescope, he would have been sorely vexed had Aristarchus presented his theory as an unalterable, indisputable fact, an *aitia*, and proposed to verify this fact through a telescopic observation of the solar system. This would not have been philosophy, but sorcery.

The ancients' whole purpose in studying the material universe can be summed up in the phrase *sozein ta phainomena*: they aimed to "save the appearances." They searched for a model — a theory or equation, a geometric or mechanical paradigm — to account for the irregularities that they observed in nature. Again, Aristarchus put forward his heliocentric hypothesis, not as a description of a physical reality, but for use in a mathematical model explaining the movements of other heavenly bodies in relation to the earth. As Professor Lloyd (1973) of Cambridge University points out, one of the major objections to the heliocentric theory in antiquity was that it failed to "save the appearances" of the stars. "If the earth moves round the sun, then there should be some variation in the relative positions of the stars observed from different points in the earth's orbit — whereas no such variation was observed in antiquity." Aristarchus tried to guard against this absence of stellar parallax by hypothesizing an infinite distance between the earth and the stars, such that no stellar parallax would be apparent.

The additional hypothesis complicated Aristarchus' explanation, however, and made it an unlikely candidate for saving the appearances. In this task, not any model would do. It had to be not only comprehensive, but simple; for the pattern underlying the cosmos was assumed to be simpler than humankind can judge. Defending the test of simplicity, Ptolemy (Lloyd 1973) wrote:

> We should try to fit the simpler hypotheses, as far as possible, to the movements in the heavens, and if this does not succeed, then any possible hypothesis. For once each of the appearances is saved as a consequence of the hypotheses, why should it still seem strange that such complications can occur in the movements of the heavenly bodies?

Ptolemy, who used epicyclic and eccentric models to save the appearances with his geocentric theory, sometimes established one hypothesis to save one set of appearances and a contradictory hypothesis to save another set of appearances. Contradiction between hypotheses did not matter, so long as each hypothesis satisfied the test of simplicity in accounting for the specific appearance of nature under investigation.

From a modern point of view, science based on attempts to save the appearances is deficient in at least two respects. First, it provides no incentive for articulating and systematizing a method of discovery (analysis) because one needs only abstract models with nonempirical hypotheses to save the appearances. Archimedes (Lloyd 1973) recognizes this deficiency in his work *On Artillery Construction*:

> It is evident that it is not possible to arrive at a complete solution of the problems involved merely by reason and by the methods of mechanics, and that many discoveries can be made only as a result of trial.

But even Archimedes' own methods of discovery seldom go beyond simple trial and error, and he is never willing to admit empirical evidence as proof of a theory.

Second, ancient science's highly theoretical character blinded it to the possibility of developing a technology. Theoretical attempts to save the appearances by neatly slipping an orderly design over the irregularities of nature naturally advanced the cause of nontechnological sciences, like astronomy and mathematics. The fixed position of the stars contrasted sharply with the flux of sublunary space, while the star patterns in the night-sky and the regular and uniform movements of other heavenly bodies suggested innumerable geometric and mathematical models. This bias against any potential technology was accentuated by the philosophical temperament of the times, wherein the mechanical and applied arts were looked upon with suspicion and scorn as labors for hands, not for minds, out of motives for monetary gain, not for knowledge. There simply was no concept of material progress or of prosperity triggered by technology, and material well-being played a minor role in ancient philosophy. Besides, an ascetic strain ran through most philosophers, or like Aristotle, they valued material prosperity only as a means to the life of virtue. Too much prosperity threatens virtue with excess, however and is as great a danger as too little.

II

Philosophy dictated, therefore, that one could *save* the appearances with hypothetical models, but one could not *know* the appearances in a manner commensurate with modern empirical proof and technological innovation. Only the nonempirical, unalterable, immanent reality could be the subject of knowledge. To know the immanent reality required a measure of imagination and a mastery of logic — both of which met in the life of virtue. Since these dictates probably inhibited scientific and material progress in ancient times, it is tempting to dismiss the view of man and of the world on which classical education is predicated. But this would be foolish. The modern world's empirical gains have, arguably, contributed to its intellectual and spiritual losses. There may be something in the attitude of the ancients worth retaining, as well as something in our modern approach in need of correcting.

What these attitudes and approaches are will become apparent if we look more closely at the scientific legacy of classical education. Since education at every level reflects man's primary assumptions about himself and his world, we begin by examining the ancients' assumptions in order to assess the role of science in their curriculum. The ancient regarded himself as a microcosm of the world he inhabited — he existed at several inner levels-of-being that paralleled the world's outer levels-of-being: (1) at the lowest level, man's physical nature, his flesh and five senses, corresponded to the material nature of the universe; (2) the rational nature of man at the next level corresponded to the law, purpose, or *logos* inherent in the material universe; (3) at the highest level, man's spiritual, mythopoeic, self-transcendent nature paralleled the divine creator, the law-giver, the form of the good standing above the material universe.

Man, according to this view, is capable of finding some species of knowledge at every level-of-being, but only at the highest level can he find true knowledge: the knowledge of himself and of his purposes. Whereas the ancients may have differed among themselves over the uses of the first two levels-of-being in attaining the third, all agreed that self-knowledge was an essential prerequisite for a correct understanding of the inferior levels. All wanted their instruction to bring man to a knowledge of his abiding self — a knowledge making man both wise and virtuous and enabling him to win insights into the lower levels of being. One fundamental principle guided this endeavor: *why* one studied, not so much *what* one studied, determined one's level of achievement. Thus does Galen (1952) the physician defend the study of the human body as one that can yield knowledge at all three levels, depending on the spirit in which it is undertaken:

Anatomical study has one use for the natural scientist who loves knowledge for its own sake, another for him who values it not for its own sake but rather to demonstrate that nature does nothing without an aim, a third for one who provides himself from anatomy with data for investigating a function, physical or mental, and yet another for the practitioner who has to remove splinters and missiles efficiently, to excise parts properly, or to treat ulcers, fistulae and abscesses.

It is, of course, the study of anatomy undertaken for its own sake that elevates man in Aristotle's Theoretic Life, or Life of Virtue, to the highest level-of-being.

The transcendent value thus ascribed to the investigation of nature should not surprise us. It is, after all, a simple extension of the reason why we credit the Greeks with inventing our modern science. Although both the Egyptians and Babylonians had developed elaborate number systems and had devised complex geometric and astronomical tables, the Milesian Greeks were the first to develop an abstract, rational system of inquiry independent of practical concerns. Man became conscious of a comprehensible logic at work in himself and in the world around him. Naturally, the physical world of buy and sell, of pain and pleasure, of graven gods and random superstitions that had blinded all previous peoples to divine reason was precisely the world that reason might help man to shuck off. Small wonder the ancients in the epoch following reason's nativity looked on his leisure moments of speculation as acts of worship!

III

The ancients' conception of parallel internal and external levels-of-being combined with their desire to save the appearances at the lower level and to transcend the appearances at the higher levels and shaped the role of mathematics in the classical curriculum. Mathematics — arithmetic, geometry, harmonics, and astronomy — saved the appearances by providing rational, abstract models to account for the irrational, concrete manifestations of a material universe. The ancients expected the study of mathematics to take their minds off the appearances and to put them on the abstract forms underlying the appearances. This abstract, rationalist tendency in their education even spilled over into the field of grammar, which the ancients studied as a pure science to learn the inherent rationality of language, not as we do today to avoid solecisms.

Mathematics, then, was meant to be a vehicle, fueled by the energy released from turning substance into form, carrying man from the lowest level-of-being toward the highest. Because mathematicians were singularly interested in the immanent forms of matter, the physical sciences made slow progress during antiquity. The exquisite mathematical symmetry assumed in nature, but often belied by nature's appearances, caused men like Pythagoras to spurn the observation of physical data and to contemplate instead the divine mind that had formed such models of symmetry and imposed them to bring cosmos out of chaos. In this way, the mathematician contributed to the Ideal Type by giving man a sense of the perfect purposes undergirding all creation and thereby putting him in touch with his perfect self — his mathematical awareness of immanent forms yielding to his consciousness of transcendent realities.

By raising arithmetic above "a squalid commercial level" (Marrou 1964) and by looking at nature with shapes and numbers, Pythagoras found evidence of a perfect, immanent reality. His evidence was not found at the empirical level of appearances, but at a higher level in the rational mind. If man can conceive of perfect triangles, Parmenides and Plato would argue, he must know more than what he sees. Following their line of reasoning, the ancients hoped to distill mathematically the aprioric forms of internal and external reality. These forms, once fully understood, would give man a knowledge of himself and of his purposes. Since such knowledge was the supreme end of a classical education, one can appreciate the ancient educator's willingness to supplement the study of language and myth with the study of mathematics. Both studies served the same end.

So long as it seeks to move man toward the highest level-of-being — saving the appearances, while promising more perfect self-knowledge — mathematics remains a unifying force in the curriculum. But as soon as it loses its classical aim and begins to serve the lowest level-of-being, mathematics also loses its integrative character and fixes a gulf between the arts and the sciences. A science of numbers feeding on technological or commercial ambitions generates a new attitude concerning the nature of man and of his purposes: it flattens the vertical levels-of-being conception of man and turns the flow of his curiosity away from the normative toward the analytical. If the study of language and myth is not washed away in this floodtide, it is left stranded on high, inaccessible ground, where it can be of little value to the education whose ends, like those of mathematics, have become wholly utilitarian. In such a setting, the mathematician is obliged to subvert the Ideal Type by convincing the student against his own better judgment of his cosmic insignificance and statistical predictability, reducing him to the level of nonliving matter.

IV

Deep down, perhaps, the ancients distrusted science. It invited specialization and a consequent imbalance in the individual and in society, while its preoccupation with unstable appearances hindered man's climb to a knowledge of the changeless immanent realities and left man open to the excesses of greed and ambition. Contrary to their modern offspring, the ancients did not believe that man could learn about himself simply by asking the same analytical questions and by applying the same empirical methods as he might in his inquiry concerning the nature of the material universe. Classical education, therefore, did not exclude science so much as it judged science of less significance than other branches of learning that promised knowledge, however slender, at higher levels-of-being. When science was studied, it was with the peculiar intention of saving the appearances: of using abstract rational models to bring irregular substance at the lowest level-of-being into line with immanent form at the higher levels.

The ancients' interest in science was what we today would call "theoretical." They asked science to enlarge their understanding of a world that in large measure they accepted as they found. But the difficulty in assigning any transcendent values to science, its restriction to intermediate rather than first and final causes, as well as the empirical limitation on its methods made it at best an adjunct to sound, responsible learning. The practical scientist was looked on with scorn unless, like Plato in the *Timaeus*, he could argue that a study of the orderly movements in the heavens helps to regularize the disorderly movements of the soul, or unless like Galen, he exemplified the Ideal Type and could defend his practice within the normative framework of his contemporaries.

Unlike Plato and Galen, however, the fathers of modern science, Bacon and Descartes, never paused to ponder scientific study's affect on man's character or to pay their respects to the Ideal Type when they boldly promised mankind a science that would make them "masters and possessors of nature." Brushing aside the question – To what end does man seek knowledge? – as teleological and therefore unsound, these original thinkers started a revolution that profoundly altered man's assumptions about himself, while dramatically expanding his opportunities for material progress.

The effects of this revolution are twofold. The first derives from Bacon's (1955) hard-edged pronouncement: "Human knowledge and power meet in one." It is, in a way, his glib response to the question – Why seek knowledge? – but the power of which he speaks is a discipline of mind leading to the manipulation of the material universe, not to the soul's salvation. With Bacon, technological science begins to replace the purely speculative science of antiquity, gradually rendering the inherited purposes of classical education as foolish. How can one argue that a training in technological science, in the means of manipulating nonliving matter, prepares a young person for the life of virtue (unless, of course, one is content – as some are – to equate a good chemist with a good person: an efficient means with a moral end)?

Whereas the modern technocrat sees knowledge as a source of power giving him a manipulative edge over nature and over others, the ancients treated knowledge as a source of virtue challenging the individual to improve himself and to look beyond the appearances for truth. Ironically, the same technology that cultivates a selfish, analytical attitude in the learner also accentuates the need for selfless, normative behavior. From the availability of birth control devices to the building of nuclear power plants to children's programming on television, modern technology confronts everyone with tremendous moral issues. Technology catches us by the collar and shouts in our face: *You* must decide! Thanks to penicillin, modern man can go a-whoring with physical impunity; thanks to mass media and new-fangled marketing techniques, he can manipulate his fellows as never before. Due to technology, never since Aristotle's day (if then) has man had so much leisure time. In short, technology has widened the sphere of our moral responsibility and increased our leisure, while undermining the normative and cultural strengths of our educational tradition.

The second effect of Bacon's revolt becomes apparent in answer to the question — What is man's justification for manipulating nature? The ideological creeds of the nineteenth century all attempt to incorporate a response, and in so doing, they complement technology in two ways. First, they flatten the ancient conception of man, confining him to the lowest level-of-being, where he is the strict sum of his physico-chemical parts. Whatever else he may appear to be, man is in fact the product of psycho-physical forces that without technology would be beyond his control. Man's defects only mirror the defects of a material universe, but modern science holds out the technological hope of a cure for these defects. Once technology has remedied the defects in man's physical environment, man will reflect a more perfect and orderly world.

Second, ideology assists technology by providing a blueprint for the more perfect and orderly world. This blueprint is predicated on theoretical models that unlike the playful hypotheses used by the ancients to save the appearances, presume both to describe things as they truly are and to imply a certain course of action. Whereas the ancients, contemplating divine ideas with pure intelligence, posited a fundamental unity in the universe, modern man, with his eyes fixed on matter, can see only a world broken up into numberless quantifiable chunks. The analytical methods of his science encourage him to go on atomizing the appearances indefinitely. Ideology, however, saves modern man from the chaos attending his methods and steps in to offer him a unifying vision of the world — a dogma based, presumably, on science rather than on philosophy or on religion. This explains the ideological tendency to elevate scientific hypotheses like Hegel's dialectic, Darwin's evolution, or Einstein's relativity to the level of dogma. While science strives to demonstrate the empirical validity of its hypotheses, ideology attempts to turn them into courses of action justifying some new manipulation of nature and of man.

This technological and ideological revolution effectively cuts modern education off from a rich classical tradition, with its prescriptive, transcendent view of man. Without this tradition the modern educator must make an ideological commitment — either consciously or unconsciously — if he expects to offer coherent learning to his students. Otherwise, the modern educator teaches them an efficiency without ends and confers on them a power to rearrange the material universe without a reason or plan for doing so. Yet whether or not he commits himself to an ideology, his students cannot escape the fate of being either Marcusian robots or random-drive bulldozers. Whichever ideology the teacher embraces, it is only a programmed replacement for classical learning, a quick catechism of answers to normative questions beyond the purview of science but not beyond the needs of the student.

V

Why, if the prospects of ideological education appear so grim, has the modern educator so consistently rejected the wisdom of the classical tradition and so uncritically accepted the pseudoscientific dogma of the nineteenth-century ideologies? Of the three reasons we shall consider, the first is rooted in man's nature. Born free or rebellious (depending on one's theology), man has always been eager to throw off the chains of the tyrannizing image and to protest (with Rousseau) his primal innocence. The evidence of man's wickedness and cruelty, however, left little doubt of his guilt; not until the advent of the great ideologies of the last century did this protest seem more than a romantic urge. But now that science has hypothesized guilt as a neurosis caused by physical forces, some as trivial as toilet training, ideology bids man to blame his angst on parents, on society, on nature, on the past, that is, on anything but himself. The Ideal Type of classical education laying on man the burden of inner change can be sloughed off.

This relieves man of responsibility: not only is his own thought and behavior beyond his control, but the direction of change in the material universe and in human events is determined and impersonal. It does not matter that the quantum physics of this century has finally discredited Newtonian determinism, insinuating an element of chance at the subatomic level. No longer accepted as a guide for composing one's life, human wisdom is limited to predicting the direction of ineluctable changes and, through technology, to making man's brief sojourn on earth as comfortable as possible. Classical normative education, full of questions of meaning and intent, purpose and significance, becomes non-sensical and vaguely disconcerting. Inherited wisdom seems an arcane and moralistic concept. The student, who was once challenged to integrate his life and his learning, is now asked to observe in detached analysis nonliving matter in the laboratory or to decipher dead words on a page.

All of this narrows the duties of the teacher considerably, thereby improving his chances for a limited success and for developing expert teaching techniques suited to his analytical methods. Ideological assumptions about man excuse the teacher from provoking his students to recognize the relation of their lessons to normative human concerns. It is difficult, as the ancients recognized, to teach science without giving the impression that man is simply a conglomeration of hydrocarbons being hurled through space signifying nothing; but classical education insisted that this appearance be saved in accordance with the aprioric forms of being. Modern ideology, however, relieves the teacher of this weighty responsibility by refusing to admit either transcendent human values or an immanent reality.

Second, ideology offers the modern educator what the classical tradition never could: a final solution. Ideology feeds on popular conceptions of science, and the breath-taking achievements of technology since the Industrial Revolution have given rise to the popular notion that solutions to all-important questions will be devised in time by science. The popular imagination, seeking a final solution in fission, in genetic engineering, or in space exploration, keeps the nineteenth-century ideologies with their Utopian prognostications alive. Meanwhile, these ideologies permit Whitehead's humble method of invention to become an omniscient end, a Wizard of Oz, from whose gadgetry all species of answers are sought. Together, the ideological future and the technological past provide the teacher with grounds for cultural optimism, despite the erosion of normative learning in the classroom. The modern educator needs ideology to bolster his implicit assumption that an analytical approach to learning adequately prepares students for the world, the life, and the final solution to come.

But his tendency to use scientific methods indiscriminately narrows the modern educator's vision. Whereas the ancients may have forfeited material progress by looking on both the knowledge of the palpable and of the impalpable as sources of virtue, modern man is in danger of falling into a gross spiritual blindness by regarding all knowledge -as a source of power. Arnold Toynbee (1962) predicts that this human habit of generalizing on successful methodologies will always end in disaster.

> Whatever the human faculty or the sphere of its exercise may be, the presumption that, because a faculty has proved equal to the accomplishment of a limited task within its proper field, it may therefore be counted on to produce some inordinate effect in a different set of circumstances, is never anything but an intellectual and moral aberration and never leads to anything but certain disaster.

This disaster is already becoming evident in our schools, where the yoke of science is thrown over all faculties of mind and spirit and where even poetry and history are taught by means of analyses that exclude imagination and normative inquiry. Yet ironically, at a time when man's power over the appearances is greatest, the possibility of his losing control over himself and his world seems highest. The better our students understand and learn to manipulate the material universe, the less they seem to know and govern themselves. Minds once used to transcend over matter become (as the deterministic ideologies on which we base our teaching insist) minds of matter. We seem destined soon to reach the fatal crossroads where the power of our technology outstrips the virtue of our self-knowledge, where our analytical knowledge of the parts sweeps away our normative grasp of the whole, where cosmos returns to chaos. Already, as E. F. Schumacher (1977) warns, the degree of bewilderment and disorientation among the young can at any moment lead to the collapse of our civilization.

The third reason for the modern educator's acceptance of ideology in place of classical education's ideals has to do with his irrepressible need to justify his vocation. One cannot teach just a collection of facts year in and year out without some justification for those facts. What, after all, is the value of teaching other than in drawing a salary if there is no value in learning other than in getting a better job? Having rejected the classical schoolmaster's belief in learning's transcendent value, the modern educator must make some other sense of his calling. He must either face the fact that education avails man of no more than enhanced power and status, or he must accept an ideological explanation fitting education into some grandiose, naturalistic scheme. The modern teacher's middle-class skepticism and intellectual disillusionment with grandiose ideological schemes, at least in America, perhaps explains his often cynical and fatalistic flight to the utilitarian alternative. If education is simply a road to the power and status of a bigger bank roll, then the teacher is naturally determined to have his share of the wealth. When he can, the modern educator abandons his calling for a commercial one, or he calls himself a professional and organizes with his colleagues to demand ever higher pay and prestige. It is hypocritical of a society that searches knowledge to find power, not virtue, and that looks to education with greedy and utilitarian eyes to refuse him.

In his book *Visions of Order*, Richard Weaver (1964) suggests that a modern teacher can only work purposefully if he is in total agreement with the goals of industrialist society because that society has invaded his classroom, expelled his dysfunctional, transcendent Ideal, revised his curriculum for its own utilitarian ends, and recreated his school in the image of the marketplace.

> The school is of course secular because a religious attitude toward the *donnee* of the world is ruled out. Questions of first and final cause are regarded as not within the scope of education, which means that education is confined to intermediate causes. Intermediate causes are of course the subject matter of science, and this attitude has the effect of orienting all education toward science. Furthermore, since industrialism is the offspring of applied science, such education fits one ideally for the industrial order. Still further, industrialism is constantly making war upon nature, disfiguring and violating her, and the products of our educational plants can be relied upon to bring the right attitude toward this work.

The school *cum* marketplace is a means to many ends, satisfying many appetites, all of them perhaps important, but none of them final, transcendent, or human. Information and skill are the commodities exchanged to prepare children for the task of maintaining our complex social and technological machinery. Not surprisingly, in the school *cum* marketplace, where education is confined to intermediate causes, students and teachers never escape being means: the one a means for the other's advancement or survival — and they treat each other as such, impersonally and professionally.

VI

At this juncture, the modern educator should be allowed an opportunity to object that classical education, whatever one wishes to say about its high-sounding intentions, is artificial and turns its back on life in order to dabble in abstractions and to invent hypothetical situations. The ancients' preference for saving the appearances with theoretical models instead of proving the appearances in controlled experiments leads inexorably, the modern educator argues, to a pedagogical habit of reaching for ideal goals, while neglecting tangible objectives well within range. Classical education, he concludes, holds experience in too low esteem — both as a means for discovering new knowledge, as well as for passing along the knowledge already in man's possession. Against this dreary portrait of classical education, the modern educator holds up today's school with its emphasis on experiential learning, where as a rule, the value of experience is never questioned and the relevance of abstract thinking always is.

What is the value of experience to learning, anyway? One's attitude toward science determines the answer. To the ancients, who expected science to save the appearances, experience for its own sake was worthless –· or worse, an experience of the unregenerate appearances might be positively detrimental, creating by emulation disharmony in the soul. One cannot in this view learn good by doing evil. The ancient schoolmaster, therefore, pursued his calling with abstract ideas, believing them to be more profitable to learning because they were more difficult to master than the concrete experience, as well as being more provocative of an immanent reality than what is usually encountered in everyday life. Handling these ideas cultivated in the student a habit of mind and a normative method of inquiry for dealing with life's everyday experiences. Most importantly, since the supreme end of learning was to form a man who conformed to a self-transcending Ideal Type, these ideas challenged the student to look beyond his own self-interest and beyond the palpable object of his direct experience in framing a solution or in making a decision.

The modern educator, on the other hand, puts much more confidence in undifferentiated experience. For instance, he is willing to let his students read just about anything, just so long as they read. This reflects his skepticism of an immanent reality and his uncanny faith that induction, even when undertaken at random, will sooner or later yield an identifiable pattern. This pattern is the knowledge he is after, and his school must simply teach the skills necessary for gathering bits and pieces of information that are supposed to emerge from such random inductions. To venture beyond this, raising questions of first and final cause or looking into the presuppositions on which pattern-recognition is based, would imply that certain experiences are more valuable than others. This the modern educator, fighting to hold onto his open, analytical mind, is loathe to do.

Modern education's leaning toward undifferentiated experiential learning begs the question of value. Not all experience is equally meaningful; in fact, no experience in itself has any value whatsoever. What validates experience are the questions, assumptions, and attitudes one brings to it and takes from it. As Aldous Huxley (1947) has written:

> Experience is not a matter of having actually swum the Hellespont, or danced with the dervishes, or slept in a doss house. It is a matter of sensibility and intuition, of seeing and hearing the significant things, of paying attention at the right moments, of understanding and

coordinating. Experience is not what happens to a man; it is what a man does with what happens to him.

A nonnormative approach to experience can teach no more than a Proustian familiarity with lost or forgotten objects — the value of the experience lying somehow hidden in how one *feels* about it. Nor does a student's analytical ability to name the flora and fauna, to describe the mating habits of monkeys, to dissect the workings of government, or to outline the plot of a novel validate his experience of these disparate objects. The value of experience relates directly to the student's aprioric knowledge of himself, of life's purposes, and of the correct choices these entail. Without the normative ability to make moral, aesthetic, and scientific judgments, a student is helpless to organize and appropriate his experience meaningfully. At best, he can, like a machine, only recollect the experience and fit it into an allegedly value-free pattern.

Normative inquiry, not analysis, renders experience valuable to mankind. Yet man's richest source of normative wisdom — his arts and letters — is often mistaught and misunderstood because of the methodical exclusion of subjects and concerns that do not lend themselves to reductive analysis. In the study of arts and letters, normative inquiry must precede and sustain analysis. What is the meaning and purpose of man's existence? What are man's absolute rights and duties? What form of government and what way of life is best? What is good, and what is evil? Not until he has explored these questions can the student begin to learn from his experiences.

Young people respond warmly and sensitively to these questions, around which the great tapestry of classical literature and art is woven. But the modern school is happier avoiding normative issues, and few old books find their way into the modern syllabus. Not only do old books raise relentless questions of value, but being rooted in a view of man antipathetic to the deterministic and "progressive" ideologies, they go on to answer these questions with an authority that seems arbitrary and abrupt. Often, the old books fall into the interstices between modern academic disciplines that were set up in the first place to facilitate analysis. When excerpts from Homer, the Bible, Dante, or Cervantes blunder into his classroom, the modern teacher affects a nonnormative pose. He employs analysis to handle the past as if it no longer held any currency, and for the sake of objectivity, he declines to take sides in the great historical conflicts and debates. He is forever reserving judgment of men and of their actions, unless they are historians with a Churchillian flair for underlining the moral lesson: for praising an Alfred, "the bright symbol of Saxon achievement, the hero of the race," or for condemning an Ethelred, "a child, a weakling, a vacillator, a faithless, feckless creature" (Churchill 1956). His small store of moral outrage he reserves for these violators of cold-blooded analysis: "subjective historians, hardcover journalists!" Not even his comparative study of religions, when he bothers, smacks of the slightest fervor for truth. "Note how Religion A borrows from Religion B on this point; note how Religion C differs in this respect from Religion A, a difference we might account for in terms of geo-political influence X." The modern teacher treats the old books like giant equations crammed with unknowns, and his duty is to factor out their normative dross with analysis, using his own choice of ideological (read *theoretical*) givens. But at him and his methods, the ancient world would have marveled, as the Peace Corps worker did when she discovered in Ghana a coastal tribe eating the fish's head and fertilizing its gardens with the body.

If the tendency to misapply science's analytical methods is bad, the impulse to confine experience to the appearances of a material universe is even worse. Whereas the ancient man's distrust of experiment matched his confidence in the immanent reality, the modern man's denial of the transcendent forces on him a narrow, materialistic definition of experience. This has the effect of excluding ex hypothesi man's individual and religious domains – in other words, an education limited to what is scientifically verifiable excludes huge tracts of human experience and sends students into the wilderness of this world without a map. So, whether he follows a Faustian determination to analyze the trans-cendent or whether he restricts learning to random inductions of palpable objects without recourse to the normative wisdom of the past, the modern educator threatens the eventual health of science, first, by hiding from himself his narrow ideological presuppositions and, second, by robbing scientific knowl-edge of human meaning and value. "The Punic power fell," according to G. K. Chesterton (1953), "because there is in . . . materialism a mad indifference to real thought. By disbelieving in the soul, it comes to disbelieving in the mind." Neither science nor civilization can survive in an atmosphere opposed to real thought and tolerant only of moral ambiguities. There is still a need – although no longer physical – to save the appearances: to make man's knowledge of the appearances answer to his normative concerns. Even in science, what is draws meaning and value from what ought to be.

6

ON THE NECESSITY OF DOGMA

> *In a civilized society, that is, one in which a common*
> *faith is combined with a skepticism about its finality,*
> *and which agrees with Pascal that "Nier, croire, et*
> *douter bien sont a l'homme ce que le courir est au*
> *cheval," orthodoxy can only be secured by a co-operation*
> *of which free controversy is an essential part.*

> *—W. H. Auden*

I

The seven liberal arts of antiquity included the four preliminary studies of arithmetic, geometry, harmonics, and astronomy, followed by the three advanced disciplines of grammar, which combined literary history and linguistic study, rhetoric, and dialectic. This curriculum passed through the Romans to the Latin West and formed the basis for the medieval *quadrivium* and *trivium*. During the Middle Ages, the *trivium* was generally taught first, with logic taking the place of dialectic. This substitution was not accidental. For an age that possessed the Truth, the dialectical search for truth was a fruitless and even frivolous, irreverent endeavor. When one knows the truth, one has no need for dialectic — all one needs is logic. Yet to an age like ours, lacking the confidence (some would say the complacency) of the early Christian era, the dialectic holds out a serious method of study imbued with a noble purpose. It is therefore to the art of dialectic that we now turn our attention.

Until now, we have mostly considered the aim of a classical education: the formation of a mature person who loves inquiry that reaches into earthly as well as transcendent realms of knowledge, who makes the connection between this knowledge and his responsibility in the life of virtue, and who struggles against long odds to fulfill in himself the high exigencies of the Ideal Type. What has been said in passing about the methods of classical learning — about the use of language and myth, the role of the teacher, and the proper attitude toward science in achieving this aim — can all be drawn together in an understanding of dialectical theory and practice. We have already seen that Socrates identified dialectic as the form of the activity of thinking — the mind's habit of challenging the thoughts and observations originating in itself or in other minds and of engaging in a desultory dialogue with itself until the issues are resolved. Most young people, for instance, go through a period of doubting or rejecting the religious, social, and political beliefs of their parents. This is healthy and indicates that their minds are coming to dialectical maturity, challenging received and fixed ideas in the process of rejecting them as extraneous or of accepting them as essential to life.

By making his students conscious of their dialectical thinking processes, Socrates hoped to assign them parts in a dramatic dialogue that otherwise occurs unconsciously and haphazardly in the thinking mind. Once the conversation between Socrates and his students deliberately took on the dialectical form of mental activity, learning became possible. Man could now visualize and oversee his own mind at work. The very form of these conversations provided Socrates' students with a model for how their minds ought to work. Whereas dialectical thinking may occur at an unconscious level in all men, education makes man conscious of how his mind works when engaged in an activity of thinking. Now, dialectic can happen more often and at higher levels. Thus, the dialectical form in which ideas are taught in a classical education provides a model for the way the mind works, as well as for the way a student will think as an adult.

Because challenges to our ideas involve our emotions and our fragile egos, most dialectical challenges come to us vaguely and unobtrusively in order to gain initial acceptance. Otherwise, we are inclined to dismiss them outright. Socrates softened his dialectical challenges by disclaiming expertise and by removing eristic emotion and egotism from the dialogue. He constantly reminded his students that he was not interested in proving them wrong or in showing himself right. Rather, he asked them simply to have patience with his "stupid questions" and to pursue their own "brilliant answers" to their logical conclusions in thought and action. His humble manner and gentle coaxing painted on the face of classical education, a wry smile that has never left it. The classical schoolmaster is still a gadfly, clothed in humor, because his task cuts across the human grain; he embraces this task knowing that only men and women who want to know the truth more than to be proven right will accept dialectical challenges and not regard reason with suspicion and fear.

"I know that I do not know" expresses Socrates' critical insight into the dialectical nature of thinking man. Although he can achieve a limited knowledge of discrete parts or a skill in performing specific tasks, man's knowledge of himself, of life's meaning and purpose, is never final or complete. Dialectic always comes out of the whole to challenge the part. Just when he grows confident of his grip on some part of knowledge, dialectic forces thinking man to recognize the inadequacy of his understanding in relation to the whole. The summit appears to recede as the climber ascends and his perspective enlarges. For dialectic, like its medium, the word, flows from a mysterious source: a unity of opposites that cannot be proven in any scientific sense but without which man cannot comprehend the things he most cares about and most profoundly experiences. Dialectic springs from the tension between being and nonbeing, identity and difference, temporal and eternal, finite and infinite, visible and invisible, rational and suprarational, the part and the whole. Without dialectic, man can know himself only as a part and the universe only as a set of parts, but with dialectic, he sees himself as a part of the whole and all parts in relation to the whole. He sees change as a part of continuity, time as a fragment of eternity, the visible as a shadow of the invisible. He throws off the exclusively analytical posture that atomizes life, smashes up experience into quantifiable chunks, names the parts but sees no connections or meanings, and would leave him splashing around in an ocean of bits and pieces one inch deep. His dialectic plunges him instead into the vasty deep, the marriage of Parmenidean unity and Heraclitean flux, the parable of the river that ever changes yet always remains the same.

The link between dialectic as a mysterious unity of opposites and dialectic as the natural activity of thinking is conscience, what G. E. Mueller (1965) calls "the dialectical core of man . . . the *daimonion* of Socrates, that inner voice of unfailing certainty which only negates." Conscience is identified with the whole of knowledge, the totality of truth. It perpetually calls man to account for what he knows: first, by stinging him when he fails to take responsibility for his knowledge and act upon it, and second, by forcing him to weigh his knowledge of himself and of his purposes and to find it inadequate and self-contradictory. Conscience negates, or challenges, man's present courses of thought and action, driving him to seek a resolution to this challenge at a higher level-of-being, where his new knowledge will in turn encounter new dialectical challenges. Conscience urges upon man the ancient injunction: Know thyself! It values not life, but the life of virtue. In the words of Socrates, "A man who is good for anything ought not to calculate the chance of living or dying; he ought only to consider whether in doing anything he is doing right or wrong – acting the part of a good man or of a bad" (Jowett 1969).

Classical education, therefore, cannot hope to achieve its lofty aims without laying great emphasis upon the development of conscience in the student. The emphasis begins, as we have seen, in the normative study of myth, from which the dogma of the Ideal Type emerges. But this should not be confused with merely inculcating a fixed code of behavior. Conscience is neither the aprioric fixed code of the religionist nor the aposterioric environmental product of the behaviorist. It is an aprioric human potential that either builds muscle or atrophies, depending upon the individual's penchant for dialectical exercise. This exercise is native to the human thinking process, although without a classical education, one is not likely to be conscious of the rules governing it. Knowing the rules and exercising regularly involve challenging in both thought and action the emerging wisdom of the myth, not with the expectation of being proven right, but with the hope of arriving through the contradiction at a higher truth. Only by wrestling dialectically with the angel of the myth, which is its dogma, its Ideal Type, can the student be blessed with a larger truth and a stronger conscience.

So much in a classical education depends on the development of conscience: the student's motivation to learn, his pleasure and understanding in reading old books and in discussing new ideas, the quality of his relation with the teacher, his ability to be objective about himself and to discover in learning a way to compose his life. The normative yeast of conscience works relentlessly in a classical education, holding the student's actions accountable to his thoughts, shuttling him back and forth between theory and practice. Conscience enforces the claims of dialectic on the student, blocking his retreat into the unreal realms of ignorance and arid analysis, ensuring that the dialectic's challenges to thought and action win a fair hearing and cause a creative tension, pushing the contradiction to a higher level of unity and self-awareness. Conscience commits the student to truth, the whole truth, establishing in him the good life, the life of virtue, and urging him to overcome his superficial, selfish, and utilitarian orientation in order to participate dialectically in the whole of knowledge.

II

So much for the theory of dialectic. In practice, dialectic begins with acceptance, not negation. It has its roots in dogma and differs widely from Cartesian learning's analytical and skeptical approach. If his subject is Plato, the student of dialectic makes Plato's thought his own, as Aristotle did, so that he can thoroughly comprehend and later transcend the Platonic wisdom. Dogma is to dialectic what doubt is to analysis: one cannot begin the one without the other. Likewise, a child cannot challenge or reject (dialectically) a parent's belief if he has not initially accepted and lived by it, nor can he transcend and resolve (dialectically) a contradiction that is simply presented to him as a naked option, a nonimperative "value preference." Dialectical learning requires that he accept a dogma before he rejects it.

In classical education, the connection between dogma and dialectic defines the master-pupil relationship. The master's life displays what it means to accept and to live by a dogma, and the pupil's imitative acceptance of his teacher's dogma affords him an insight into his own life and studies that eventually corroborates, refines, or invalidates the dogma. The pupil's initial acceptance of the teacher's or the myth's dogma lays the groundwork for his intellectual and moral growth, so long as the dogmatic content of his education is always subjected to dialectical challenges.

Today, however, teachers are discouraged from teaching themselves, and students are asked to judge ideas in analytical detachment on the basis of unverifiable ideological presuppositions. In this regard, Descartes is the architect of the modern school. He used doubt as a proof of being and thereby paved the way for modern education's rejection of the dialectical unity of opposites, whether of mind and body, of visible and invisible, or of doubt and dogma. Yet ironically, there is an unverifiable presupposition lurking behind Descartes' first principle, the *cogito ergo sum*. By attributing thought to being, Descartes makes an hypothesis that is not itself subjected to doubt. Thought is not a proof of being (it is a proof of thinking), but that it should be so is a dogma necessary for the birth of Cartesian rationalism. What in fact the *cogito ergo sum* demonstrates is man's inability to doubt in the absence of a dogma attributing thought to being — a dialectical verity! Dialectic adheres even to the little grain of indubitable truth that Descartes presumes to have found. Indeed, all knowledge of first and final causes in which man defines himself and his purposes begins with dogma, not with doubt, and feeds on itself dialectically. Man's knowledge is without value to him unless he reaches it dialectically — unless it animates his body, indwells his mind, and possesses his soul.

All of life is the student's laboratory for dialectical learning. *Dogmas* — from the Greek meaning "that which seems good" — are his hypotheses. He seldom chooses them; they are thrust upon him by his teachers, by the old writers, or by the very nature of life itself. The obvious example, as Kant pointed out, is the dogma of free will underlying all human behavior. No one has ever scientifically verified free will, nor has the dogma ever relaxed its grip on the average man seeking to carve out a moral and purposeful life, despite the attacks levied against it by deterministic philosophers in the name of experimental science. Dogmas like free will are not value preferences or moral options, but firm convictions received on authority, since dialectic begins with sincere acceptance, not skeptical detachment. Once he receives a dogma, the student of dialectic begins in his life and learning to verify it. At the same time, challenges and contradictions to the dogma occur, altering the original dogma, reformulating it. Conscience compels the student to act on these reformulations, to take responsibility for what he knows, and to be constantly renewing his dialectical quarrel with life and letters. Rather than prepare the student for the carefree outer life he wants, dialectical learning awakens him to the 'quarrelsome' inner life he must have if he is to preserve and enlarge his frail humanity.

Dialectic's modern antagonist complains that a negating dialectic lacks precision, while subjecting man to a life of unceasing challenges; but the advantage of dialectic over modern analysis, despite its comparative sloppiness, is its nondefinitive yet dogmatic acceptance of the totality of human experience in all its domains — individual, social, and religious. Dialectic alone teaches man what he must know to achieve full humanity: his obligations to himself, to others, and to God. This is possible because dialectic, unlike the analytic, is not bound to a Cartesian or utilitarian presupposition about reality. It can introduce questions of value, of judgment and discernment, and of first and final causes — all fundamental to normative education. Its limitations at the lowest level-of-being are of course obvious, but at least it does not insist on reducing man's nature to the level of nonliving matter in the interest of achieving a pointless certainty or probabilistic precision. Dialectic, despite its scientific and linguistic limitations, remains man's best educative chance for tapping the knowledge of himself and of his purposes, for passing this knowledge on from one generation to the next, for repairing and developing conscience, and, eventually, for ascribing human value to science and for asserting normative control over technology. "The slenderest knowledge that may be obtained of the highest things," wrote the Aristotelian theologian, Saint Thomas Aquinas (1955), "is more desirable than the most certain knowledge obtained of lesser things."

Dialectical education implies that a learner cannot see all sides of a question until he has chosen one, but analytical education assumes that choosing one side blinds the learner to all others. In analysis, therefore, the learner cannot be held responsible for his knowledge because the means for making him responsible lie in an untouched set of moral or intellectual options. Adopting one option means ignoring all the others. Conscience plays no role. Thought and action exist apart from each other, the mind affecting to observe but not to participate in the acting out of ideas, fearful lest its participation should prejudice learning, yet ignorant that participation is essential in bringing together thought and action for responsible learning. For this reason, the value-free approach of analysis warps education by methodically straining out the normative nutrition in life and letters and by sacrificing the transcendent, life-transforming value of knowledge to a dead set of utilitarian options and objectives. Whereas the value-free stance is useful in analysis at the low material level-of-being, it is a disastrous position to try to live from.

Nevertheless, modern education has chosen to disguise its need for dogma by subjecting all content to doubt, while granting analytical form the status of an incontrovertible dogma. When a methodology thus becomes a dogma, what happens? We can find an answer in the past. Ironically, the modern era, so proud of its enlightenment, has chosen in this regard to base its education on a method producing a vast multiplicity of parochial concerns. Today, we count quarks and pulverize DNA molecules instead of numbering demons on the heads of pins, but what has really changed? We still flounder in a shallow ocean of bits and pieces, of endless taxonomies. Can there be an end to dredging up the particles of the material universe? What is it that we are actually looking for? Do we seek a palpable divinity dancing under our microscopes? What does it all mean to man and to how he composes his life?

This last is the fundamental question of our times, yet it is a question that modern reductionist education refuses to address, since it lacks not only an answer, but even the most rudimentary methods for seeking an answer. We have embraced a methodology that by its very nature frustrates our normative questions, and we must watch helplessly the pathetic attempts of people trained only in scientific analysis to answer normative questions at the heart of their humanity. In their confusion, they often try to adapt science to their nonscientific questions, turning to astrology, the I Ching, biorhythms, pyramid power, popular psychology, and all that; but these choices produce neither science nor self-knowledge — only a flight into the irrational and absurd.

What is the value of a method of looking at reality that arms man with an awful power over the material universe but offers not the slightest hint of how such power ought to be wielded, nay, that positively discourages the raising of normative questions and, thereby, divorces man's knowledge from his responsibility? The value of analysis is limited, to be sure, for it cannot address the normative questions successfully. Many modern schools in vague alarm, however, insist that it make an attempt to do so in seminars on values clarification and value preference and in classes on ethics, where all the "moral options" are trotted out with eerie disinterest or picked over with nauseating, utilitarian self-interest. But all of this misplaced use of analysis is precisely why the dialectic must wrest control of our schools from the analytical: to save science from a perversion of its methods and applications and man from a species of knowledge that means nothing to him personally. "Better not to know," writes T. S. Eliot (1939) in *The Family Reunion*, "than to know the fact and know it means nothing."

III

Although dialectic is the obvious choice for our modern schools, the utilitarian demands of a technological society are so great and the vested interests of analysis so pervasive that a general revolution in education is out of the question. Modern educators are more interested in teaching what they can measure and in "covering the material" than in an education whose form and content have an intangible, transcendent value. Moreover, few modern teachers understand dialectic, although like all people, they spend most of their lives dwelling on normative questions and obscurely seeking dialectical answers. Perhaps an example from the classroom will help bring the nature of this misunderstanding into focus.

Recently, I visited a class of 14-year-olds about to embark on a study of Plato's *Meno*. The teacher chose Plato, he told me, because he wanted his students to read something that would provoke them to make a connection between what they study in school and how they behave and see themselves outside the school. Being a classicist, he knew that classical literature makes it difficult for a teacher to obfuscate or for a student's analysis to avoid the writer's normative designs. From the beginning, however, this teacher's unintentionally analytic approach to the *Meno* thwarted his goal. He had given his class the text straight away, asking them to outline the argument: "What is virtue? Can it be taught? List in logical sequence Meno's questions and assertions and Socrates' responses." The next day, the students returned, having broken down the dialogue into its parts, but they were confused and unmoved by the argument.

What went wrong? The teacher discovered that a seemingly innocuous analysis had subverted his best intentions and obscured Plato's classic dialogue. The students' understanding of virtue, having been drawn strictly from analysis, was superficial and detached. They had failed to participate dialectically in the struggle of ideas; yet they hoped to fob off their research as thought — a common fault of analytical learning that touches every level of modern education. The teacher decided, therefore, to approach the question of virtue without a text, as Socrates himself would have, asking his students to define virtue as they found it in themselves or in someone they admired. The next day in class, they debated with some fervor their dogmatic definitions of virtue. As they argued among themselves, one began to feel the old charisma of the Ideal Type filling the room.

The following day, the teacher attempted to draw the parents of his students into the dialectical web. He requested his students to elicit from their parents an answer as to whether virtue can be taught. (It was revealing to learn later how few parents had ever asked themselves this question or articulated an answer, yet what question could be more pertinent to raising a child?) In the end, not until he had his students' full involvement in the question and commitment to an answer — not until every student had articulated and defended a dogma on virtue — did the teacher reintroduce the text, this time not in an analytical attempt to pick apart Plato's argument, but in an effort to grasp the truths of the classic in accordance with the needs and the dogmas of his pupils. Nor was this difficult once their respective dogmas gave them each a role in the Platonic drama of ideas.

The pressure to teach everything by means of analysis does not originate exclusively in the maths and sciences. In practice, the teacher often becomes so caught up in getting his students to cover a body of material that he forgets why they are studying it. Analysis assures the teacher that the material is being covered (that his students did read the *Meno*: their outlines prove it) and will be easily tested. Analysis frees the teacher from the need to make a personal commitment to ideas. This *laissez-faire* attitude toward ideas releases both the student and teacher from taking active responsibility for what they know. Parents and administrators, fearing the controversial influences of idiosyncratic teachers, encourage this careless analytical attitude — ignorant that dogma is not *the* answer but *an* answer necessary for initiating classical (that is, dialectical) learning.

The great teacher, in fact, is necessarily dogmatic in the sense of being committed to ideas. He reaches the wills of his students, as well as their minds. Truly, he knows the futility and danger of gaining the one without the other. The noble intention of his teaching, like that of all great literature and art, is the antithesis of pornography: to move his students to will a moral act, as opposed to an immoral one. The great teacher shares with Cicero and the rhetorical tradition of Isokrates the conviction that life and letters reflect the normative truths and moral imperatives immanent within nature and within language. Whatever fails to evoke and develop a lively conscience in himself and in his students is, so far as he is concerned, banal, mediocre, devoid of style, and empty of meaning and value.

IV

It may be that the modern misunderstanding of true dialectic stems from an unwitting acceptance of its popular materialist perversion. Historians a hundred years from now will probably expend much ink trying to explain one of the chief ironies of our times: on the one hand, the West's passionate rejection of what in Communist doctrine most appeals to the ideals of community in its Christian-humanist tradition and, on the other hand, its whole-hog acceptance of the one fundamental tenet of Communism most repellent to its tradition. I refer to the tenet of dialectical materialism. Traditionally, Western man has heard the call demanding inner change and has assumed freedom as his reward for shouldering the responsibility of heeding this call. Socrates' dialectic made him capable of inner change by moving him toward the highest level-of-being, where he transcended physical limitations and attained full humanity — a state summarized by Kazantzakis' epitaph: "I expect nothing. I am not afraid. I am free." Dialectic formed a man who both knew and desired what he knew, and Western education affirmed until recently this connection between intellect and will as vital to the individual's freedom and dignity.

Whereas Socrates' dialectic was man's mountain path to knowledge and self-awareness at the highest level-of-being, Marx and his followers borrow from Hegel, whose dialectic is a law of contradiction and reconciliation operating in human history. Marx's dialectic emphasizes the individual's social class rather than his thought processes. Self-knowledge is no longer transcendent, but derivative. People become the product of their class and of the part they play in the class struggle. Normative questions wear utilitarian garb, for a person's value and meaning is not a function of his self-awareness or of his allegiance to the pattern of truth represented by an Ideal Type, but of his political role in the emerging social order. The dialectical materialist turns man into a means, and a negligible means at that. He is merely a pawn of historical processes, fired perhaps by vain ambitions to become a bishop or a knight, and with a limited capacity (largely determined by birth) to choose the winning side. His own thinking, the Socratic dialectic, being largely determined, counts for nothing.

Although Western man has seldom lived without a fondness for material comfort and well-being, he has not previously identified matter with the whole range of human experience, the totality of truth, and sought to understand, manipulate, and accumulate matter for its own sake. That he has begun to do so, and thereby denied his tradition's levels-of-being conception of man, is more the observation than the result of Marx's writings. Marx concludes from this observation that man can only know himself as a sensed object and that the sensed object is the limit of man's desire. All abstractions, all ideals, and all beliefs only mask man's desire to master or possess the sensed object; the desire itself arises out of social situations, which are, in turn, the product of specific material conditions. "For me," writes Marx (Feuer 1959) in *Das Kapital*, "the ideal is nothing other than the material after it has been transposed and translated inside the human head." Man's intellect, therefore, is harnessed to the sole purposes of material struggle and physical survival, and the aim of education becomes similarly utilitarian: to pass on to each member of the next generation the analytical tools he will need to know himself as a sensed object within the social and political domains of human experience and to function effectively within those domains. Man's individual and religious domains are dismissed as intellectual fantasies, dreamworlds, "the material after it has been transposed and translated inside the human head."

Mao Tse-tung, perhaps the most sophisticated of the Communist theorizers, explains how the materialist premises of Marx's dialectic affect education. "Dialectics in the proper sense," Mao (1968) quotes Lenin, "is the study of contradiction in the very essence of objects." For Mao, however, the essence of objects is no demiurge of the real world, no immaterial immanent spirit, but it is the physical property of the object itself — proton and electron, if you will. Contradiction is the universal law of the material universe, whether manifest in the historical struggle between capitalism and socialism or in the magnetic tension fusing an atom. At any given moment, one aspect of the contradiction is primary, the other secondary. All change in these aspects is quantitative and proceeds in slight increments. All *true* change in objective reality is rendered by these quantitative increments, whereas *apparent* change — Mao's expression for the qualitative — merely records a sudden change in the balance between the two aspects of the contradiction caused by the accumulation of quantitative increments in one aspect and not in the other. Imagine dropping pebbles onto the lighter tray of Libra's scales until the lighter tray overtakes the heavier, and the balance shifts. The shift represents the *apparent* change occurring when the secondary aspect of a contradiction overtakes the primary aspect, thereby establishing a new contradiction. Thus does Mao dismiss the appearance of a qualitative effect. Similarly, he dismisses qualitative cause by describing it as a material influence beyond the reckoning or control of the apparent agent. So, whether one wishes to produce causes or to predict effects, a quantitative knowledge of objective reality is the key. Only by knowing the material universe's affect on man and by learning how to manipulate it in order to guide its influences can man achieve a limited, if precarious, freedom from being manipulated himself.

Mao belongs in our discussion of education because, in many respects, he best articulates and defends the modern educator's position. With Mao, the modern educator believes that his students' welfare and freedom will depend on their precarious ability to manipulate the material universe, to perform complicated tasks, and to cope with the complexities of life in modern industrial society. To provide the requisite skills is the objective of his modern school, and little thought is wasted on the transcendent ends these skills were meant to serve before dialectic was corrupted by Hegel and Marx and their followers. For instance, the inability of the present generation of young people to read, write, and think is only a symptom of our departure from dialectical learning, but it is everywhere being treated as the disease itself. So long as these skills are valued only for utilitarian ends, such as those delineated by Mao, they must fail to excite in our youth the efforts necessary for their mastery. Not until we once again recognize and articulate the transcendent value of sound thinking, wide reading, and lucid writing will our students respond to their lessons enthusiastically.

Underlying the modern educator's preference for utilitarian learning is another assumption he shares with dialectical materialism. Show me a mechanic, Marx would argue, and I will show you a man who thinks like a mechanic, defines his purposes and ends like a mechanic, and sees the world as only a mechanic can. In other words, regardless of what a child learns in school, his vocation in life will determine his responses to the normative questions. Whereas Aristotle's education assumed his students' future leisure and taught them how to use it, the modern educator — assuming the psychological enslavement of the proletariat — would teach his students how to acquire more leisure without presuming to tell them how to use it. There is an appealing logic in all this, and at a time of rapid educational expansion into the traditional working classes and of increasing technological demands at every level of employment, this logic allows the educator to brush aside the normative emphasis of classical education and urge the school to pursue blatantly utilitarian ends.

The flaw in this logic is that we are not dealing with a simple verifiable description of a particle of brute matter, but with an ideology that poisons free thought by arbitrarily restricting our consideration of man to only one of his three domains, the social-political, while disregarding the individual and the religious domains of human experience. Yet we discuss this social-political animal with a language and objectivity that resounds of scientific verifiability, logically deducing all manner of conclusions from a one-dimensional man. Even if it could be substantiated that all mechanics are conservative Democrats or card-carrying Communists, who would be so brash as to suggest that all mechanics hold congruent convictions about themselves and about God?

By restricting man's experience to the material universe and his knowledge of himself to the social-political domain, dialectical materialism presents an ideology almost wholly compatible with the fashion of modern Western thought. This thought subverts Western man's long tradition of dialectic by ignoring the eternal, invisible, transcendent parts of the whole and by replacing provisional dogmas with an ironclad ideology. Without acknowledging the whole, however, there can be no unity of opposites, only bewilderment and disorientation; without accepting dogma, there can be no beginning of dialectic and no binding relation between the idea and the deed, between learning and life. The pedagogical avoidance of dialectic and dogma and of whatever touches man in his individual and religious domains forfeits the possibility for a truly classical education. Whereas Socrates' dialectic embraced the whole and encouraged a struggle between the normative and utilitarian and between the dialectical and the analytical, modern ideology declares the struggle ended by peremptorily deciding the issue in favor of the utilitarian and analytical. Eventually, utilitarian and analytical learning veers into irresponsible selfishness and clinical detachment — a vicious combination of traits, for which the twentieth century provides more than its share of *exempla*, beginning with Hitler and Stalin and ending with the epidemic of addiction, intimidation, and malaise infecting our own children.

Francis Bacon's often-quoted dictum comes to mind: "If a man will begin with certainties, he shall end in doubts; but if he will be content to begin with doubts, he shall end in certainties." But what sort of certainties will doubt afford a man in the end, and what will their true worth to him be? Following Descartes, man did begin with doubt, and he has ended, as Bacon prophesied, in certainties: ideological certainties. Perhaps the old way of beginning with dogma and ascending a dialectical staircase to an upper room of fragile truths and intangible beliefs was not so bad after all. At least it threw open the windows of inquiry on all of man's domains and provided him with a means of gaining knowledge about the things he held most dear and experienced most profoundly. It repaired his conscience, taught him to live better, and restored his humanity. "It encouraged a philosophical approach to life's troublesome questions," as John Gardner (1977) characterized Chaucer's early education as having done, "and gave noble and dignified arguments on the meaning of life and death."

7

THE ENNOBLING OF THE MASSES

Do you wish to give a certain elevation to the human mind, and teach it to regard the things of this world with generous feelings, to inspire men with a scorn of mere temporal advantages, to form and nourish strong convictions, and keep alive the spirit of honorable devotedness? Is it your object to refine the habits, embellish the manners, and cultivate the arts, to promote the love of poetry, beauty, and glory? Would you constitute a people fitted to act powerfully upon all other nations, and prepared for those high enterprises which, whatever be their results, will leave a name forever famous in history? If you believe such to be the principle object of society, avoid the government of the democracy.

—Alexis de Tocqueville

I

Education in ancient times was aimed at a small elite, and classical education has never shaken the charge of being elitist. Its ideals are often said to be irrelevant to the conditions and requirements of life in an industrial democracy. A number of notable classical scholars — Nietzsche, Bergson, and Max Scheler on the Continent, F. R. Leavis and Brooks Otis in Great Britain and the United States — have complicated the issue by using Plato's critique of democracy to support their case for the recognition and formation of educated elites. Democracy's stampeding masses will destroy themselves and trample down their beloved liberties — so the argument goes — if they are not led by an elite of learned men and women. These scholars build their argument for educating small elites on the same footing of social and political exigency as those who think all classical education an aristocratic impertinence. Both groups define man in social-political terms, and both agree that modern technological society requires a horde of technicians to keep its machinery running smoothly and its denizens well-housed and well-fed.

The classical scholars, however, recognize that material efficiency may make life possible, but it does not make society civilized or life worth living, nor is it alone capable of preserving the democratic ideals. There must be some nobler purpose and a higher sense of value infusing society's material efficiency and informing the common people, whose lives are consumed in the daily contest for material well-being. An educated elite is in their view needed to preserve and develop culture: the innumerable artistic, literary, political, religious, and social means of articulating society's purposes and values. This seems a harsh view perhaps, but before rejecting it, we must fairly consider the problem. With the increasing demands of the marketplace and of the state on education, added to the mounting strain placed on the school by the disintegration of the family, can modern education any longer hope to prepare the custodians of culture while training millions of needed technicians? If not, is it necessary or possible for a few to preserve and develop culture for the many?

To this last question, no less a democrat than Thomas Jefferson agreed on both counts that it was necessary and possible to make an elite responsible for culture. He tried to resolve the obvious inequity of this solution by distinguishing between what he called the "artificial" and the "natural" gentleman. Sharing the presuppositions of the scholarly elitists, Jefferson thought that culture in a democratic society depended on the recognition of an elite that would inherit its cultural responsibilities from its parents, as well as on the formation of an elite which would share these responsibilities because of its native abilities. In a neat synthesis of the rhetorical and philosophical traditions, Jefferson expected classical education to prepare the artificial and natural elites by implanting responsible learning in the one and by eliciting it from the others.

Jefferson's elitist mythology was fine so long as the technical needs of the country remained modest and could be handled by a system of apprenticeship rather than of education. But the modern democrat will point out that the formal schooling of the patriarch's day was an exception, not the rule, which two centuries of educational reform have changed. The needs of the modern industrial state are no longer those of the youthful republic, and the distinction between artificial and natural gentlemen sounds as quaint as Plato's elitist myth of the gold, silver, and bronze classes. Today's democrat asks instead: Who will select the cultural elite, and on what basis? At what level will the education of this elite begin? How will the elite benefit the masses in the fulfillment of its cultural responsibilities, and how will it be compensated? In the end, what will prevent a hiatus from developing between those whose social task is utilitarian and those whose task is normative? What will stop the presumption of superiority from cropping up on one side or on the other?

While the modern democrat — misled by much classical scholarship, as well as by his liberal aristocratic forebears — snipes at the elitist mythology with these questions, his utilitarian countryman charges the citadel of classical education head-on, asking: Of what value to society is an elite culture anyway? How does culture further the chief ends of modern industrial democracy, ensuring prosperity, security, and equal opportunity for all? How does culture help the individual put bread on the table and keep him off the welfare rolls? How does culture prepare him for the complications of day-to-day living in a highly bureaucratized, technological society? In truth, it does not, and classical education is overrun while trying to defend itself in these utilitarian terms. The modern democrat, already justly suspicious of the elitist myth, joins his utilitarian countryman in rejecting the elitist thesis, along with the idea of a classical education on which it is unreasonably predicated.

II

The scholarly elitists rightly assign classical education the mission of preserving and developing culture, but they undermine the role of classical education in democracy by supporting their arguments for an educated elite from models of aristocratic government. Like Athenian philosophers, they cast longing eyes on distant Sparta, but their arguments neglect the happy political realities right under their noses. In fact, the elitists are foolish to assume that culture can be cultivated for the many by the few in a democratic state. The very notion denies the essential elements of democracy, while introducing into the heart of democracy a controlling aristocratic interest. Yet because they refuse to exchange their aristocratic presuppositions for democratic ones, the elitists cannot admit the democratic logic of extending classical education to all. Their refusal coincides conveniently with the utilitarian's persistent unwillingness to risk the loss of a job-trained citizenry by opening up classical education to the laboring masses.

The logic of democracy, however, demands that everyone be educated as members of an elite. Each student in a democracy must be educated as an aristocrat. Democracy assures him of the unique privileges of an aristocrat: the freedoms of thought, expression, movement, and worship, as well as the rights to own property and to have a voice in framing the laws by which he and his children will be governed. The industrial democratic state has in effect made each of its citizens an Aristotelean aristocrat, by extending to him leisure by way of technological advancement and political power by way of universal suffrage. Education, therefore, must impress on the citizen a lively sense of the responsibilities attending these privileges: his responsibility to the past, his obligation to govern and discipline himself, to contribute in every way he can to the preservation and development of his society's purpose and sense of values, his duty to love the law and to carry himself before his compatriots in an exemplary manner, and the opportunity to use his leisure for the realization of his marvelous human potentials. In theory, democracy puts Aristotle's "good life," the life of virtue, within reach of every man; but only a classical education is designed to turn this theory into practice, while safeguarding democracy with a norm-minded citizenry by extending culture to all.

Plato notwithstanding, democracy is the noblest experiment in government because, against great odds and perils, it frees all men to develop their full human potentials. The imperiling contradiction lies between a utilitarian Scylla — the fear that freedom will lead to disorder, inefficiency, and a loss of means — and an elitist Charybdis — the concern that universal privilege will degenerate into general irresponsibility, lawlessness, decadence, and a loss of ends. Only with a norm-minded citizenry, the product of a broadly based classical education, can the democratic ship of state negotiate a safe passage. This, indeed, is the boast of Pericles (Thucydides 1973) in the Funeral Oration: that the education of the Athenians had allowed each of them to attain his full human potential, making Athens in turn an education to all of Greece.

> Taking everything together then, I declare that our city is an education to Greece, and I declare that in my opinion each single one of our citizens, in all the manifold aspects of life, is able to show himself the rightful lord and owner of his own person, and do this, moreover, with exceptional grace and exceptional versatility.

The Athenian's city was like a school to him, and Pericles was the perfect teacher. He did not merely bend to the will of the people or appeal to their baser instincts to win their approval, but he educated and shaped his countrymen by challenging them dialectically. His unpopular Peloponnesian War strategy demonstrated the educative role of the statesman, whose ability to lead people toward an objective they do not know they want to reach parallels the dogmatic role of the classical teacher. Moreover, Pericles lived his lessons and taught himself, his renowned moderation and evasion of praise and glamour affording an example of the Ideal Type to his countrymen.

Since the entire free citizenry of the democracy was involved in this education, *paideia* — the Greek word meaning both "culture" and "education" — was not for some elite to preserve and develop. It was the property of every citizen, a natural right, which he was obligated to practice, to protect, and to pass on. He never asked: Of what use is *paideia* to me? The truly educated person never does. He knows to what degree *paideia* has opened to him the knowledge of himself and of a full life within all the domains of his humanity. He appreciates the fact that *paideia* is the state's gift to him, not simply his obligation to the state: it is his unique opportunity in a democracy to achieve a full and rich humanity. The modern debate over whether classical education is elitist, useless, or unbecoming to a democracy misses this point. The debaters adopt an incomplete view of man, each making him a means in relation to the state: the elitist seeing him as a custodian of the state's culture; the utilitarian seeing him as a technician in the state's economy. By assuming man to be only a social-political animal, who acts exclusively out of self-interest with no normative knowledge, the elitist values culture as a glittering social adornment, while the utilitarian insists that culture prove its worth in service to the state. But the debate is of no interest to the individual who knows himself also as an end in relation to the state, and whose responsibility toward himself and toward God is arbitrarily excluded from the terms of the debate.

Democratic society needs a citizen body educated to make normative decisions — decisions about what ought to be as well as what can be. Otherwise, the culture from which democracy derives its sustaining purposes and sense of values becomes helpless to defend itself against the utilitarian onslaught of citizens who think *paideia* to be elitist and useless. Lacking a normative education, these citizens are already confused about themselves and their needs, and they will spurn the appeals of any pseudoaristocratic elite urging on them a set of individual and religious norms that make no sense to mere social-political animals. Citizens without classical education will prove, as they did in ancient Rome, that whether democratic societies have cultural elites is a moot question. In a democracy, the purposes and sense of values cultivated by a few will not for long be able to provide direction and meaning for the many, who control policy directly with their votes and society indirectly with their appetites. In the end, elite culture will be rejected in favor of a "bread and circuses" perversion of culture — a life of pleasure being the only utility a nonnormative citizen body can appreciate.

Nor will the abolition of classical education solve the problem of elites for the modern democrat. The nonnormative education of the utilitarian's Utopia is never in reality value free; it simply replaces the prescriptive and transcendent values of the classical tradition with a new set of materialistic values. These new values create economic elites and may even usher in a brief period of prosperity, albeit at the expense of man's sense of his and his fellows' individual and religious worth. In the long run, society is no better off for having rid itself of the "elitist" scourge of classical education. The greater abundance flowing into society from the formation of the economic elites seems only to aggravate man's sense of anxiety, dissatisfaction, alienation, and disorientation. The snobbishness and banality of the new elites contrast woefully with the old classically educated elite's ethic of service to the community and of commitment to self-transcending ideals. Meanwhile, the hapless democrat, who had hoped to escape the cloying noblesse oblige of an aristocratic elite, falls into the clutches of an irresponsible and selfish economic elite.

Classical education is neither wedded to an aristocratic form of government (as the scholarly elitist presupposes) nor is it the pestiferous breeding ground for elites (as the modern democrat fears). Rather, classical education meets the conditions and requirements of the whole man, developing his individual, social, political, and religious selves — and when extended through the blessing of democracy to the masses, classical education gains in strength and in richness, as the limited example of Periclean Athens attests. To speak of classical education for the few is a contradiction in terms, for *paideia* is the inheritance of all men as individuals, not of any class of men as servants to the state. In turn, universal classical education, like universal suffrage, benefits the state unintentionally, while serving the individual. What the state may lose in efficiency and in single-minded direction is more than compensated by the superabundant energies released by democracy. What the state forfeits in skilled workers, it more than recovers through classical education's formation of a norm-minded, self-governing citizenry in which, as Pericles declared, "each single one of [the] citizens, in all of the manifold aspects of life, is able to show himself the rightful lord and owner of his own person, and do this, moreover, with exceptional grace and exceptional versatility" (Thucydides 1973). This is utility with a vengeance!

III

What, then, are the objectives of universal classical education in a democracy? First, it responds to the conditions and requirements of the whole man in all his domains — the individual, the social and political, and the religious. Classical education's normative approach to learning makes this response, integrating the individual by bringing his domains into balance. Only the balanced, norm-minded individual will cheerfully accept responsibility for the state without feeling imposed upon by it. He will realize that his need for the state complements the state's need of him and that the development of his full human potential depends on an active acknowledgment of his obligations to himself, to his neighbors through the state, and to God. This is the theme of Socrates' remarks to Crito and the essential justice of Plato without the severe stratification of the *Republic*: the belief that the individual's harmony of parts redounds to the glory and benefit of the state. The state reflects the just man (the man whose parts are in balance) because his participation in the state is alone what balances, justifies, and legitimizes the state.

Classical education's second objective in a democracy is to teach people to discriminate and to make sound judgments. True democrats invariably want to know not only how, but why. They want to know not only how an analysis is made, but what it means. They want to know not only if a thing can be done, but if it ought to be done. Standing between them and their need to possess this knowledge are two conditions. The first condition is a free access to ideas and to a high quality of information on which to base informed opinions, and the second is a normative intellect, embodying a clear definition of purposes and a discriminating sense of values with which to synthesize this information and form intelligent judgments. Lacking either of these conditions, democracy will fail because its average citizen will begin to doubt the soundness of his own judgments. He will surrender his fundamental democratic right to ideas and to decision making to a few experts whose specific job it is to analyze a specific issue and decide the issue, as an analyst might say, on its own merits. Not only does this separate the citizen from specific policy issues, but it makes overall policy fragmentary, self-contradictory, and incomprehensible. Yet without classical education's normative learning, the democratic citizen will grow lazy in his demand for a high quality of public thought and information. He will doubt his ability to decide the issues shaping his life, and he will take another step beyond representative government in relinquishing the privilege of self-government by putting himself at the mercy of a few experts. At last, abandoning their Western classical heritage, they will resign themselves and their children to an Asian democracy, that is, a democracy in name only.

Third, classical education in a modern democracy teaches a person to value the aims of government more than its forms. This is an important lesson, not easily learned by the democratic youth. All forms of government, including democracy, market their own brands of tyranny, which threaten learning by becoming part of the routine of the classroom. Take, for instance, the trendy notion that since all men and women are different and since each individual has a right to be himself or herself, education must be "tailored" to the desires and needs of the individual. This view, which is consistent with the utilitarian and reductionist orientation of modern education, has a canonical hold on the American school. To insist that all students receive a classical education would — according to this view — deny their important differences and desecrate the sacred forms of democracy. It does not matter that this notion stresses man's formal differences at the expense of his fundamental similarities, while it smites the industrial democratic state just where it is most vulnerable. The forces to which democracy naturally gives encouragement accentuate the differences existing in society and assist in the rise of minority and special interest politics, in the growth of academic and vocational specialization, in the fragmentation of knowledge, in the breakup of the family, and in the proliferation of creeds and cults. Industrial democracy's centrifugal pressure on the human community emphasizes the need for a universal classical education binding young people together in understanding and pursuit of the great human values and aims they all share.

But in a democracy, tyranny enters the classroom by declaring education's freedom from the dogma, the authority, and the tradition of a classical education. The classroom is expected to mirror democratic society, the home of such declarations, and to provide for the democratic youth a pleasant, free, and happy setting with just enough restraint to ensure a modicum of order. Eventually, in this blissful setting, where everyone finds encouragement to study only what interests him, the democratic tyranny of the group manifests itself. The group dictates to the individual the "acceptable" level of his commitment to ideas; it controls the climate of learning and the intention and will of the learner; and in the absence of the Ideal Type, it erects a tyrannizing image of its own adolescent design.

More tyrannies follow. Where democratic forms are deemed valuable regardless of the aims of education, disinterested analysis drives normative inquiry out of the classroom and severs the vital umbilicus between knowledge and responsibility. In the impartial eye of analysis, all aims appear of equal value, and no aim can lay claim on the learner's will. If it did, it would subvert the freedom that he values for its own sake, as well as prevent the detachment necessary for an "objective" analysis. So, in the name of freedom, a reductionist method restricts the quest for knowledge in the democratic classroom, and the democratic youth methodically rejects the dogmas of normative learning in a manner recorded by Plato (Jowett 1969) in Book VIII of the *Republic*:

> If any one says to him that some pleasures are the satisfactions of good and noble desires, and others of evil desires, and that he ought to use and honor some and chastise and master others — whenever this is repeated to him he shakes his head and says that they are all alike, and that one is as good as another.

For the educator in this scenario, only those forms of learning that guarantee maximum freedom — democracy and scientific analysis — retain an unquestioned value. The educator resists defining the aims of his school, except with vague and fatuous generalizations, because aims condition freedom, predicating it on certain higher values. This in a school where the forms of freedom are sinc qua non is of course unthinkable. So the aimless tyranny of a value-free analysis continues, supported by democracy in the classroom, and the democratic youth is led into the anarchy of a "distracted existence," living

> from day to day indulging the appetite of the hour; and sometimes he is lapped in drink and strains of the flute; then he becomes a water-drinker, and tries to get thin; then he takes a turn at gymnastics; sometimes idling and neglecting everything, then once more living the life of a philosopher; often he is busy with politics, and starts to his feet and says and does whatever comes into his head; and, if he is emulous of anyone who is a warrior, off he goes in that direction, or if of men of business, once more in that. His life has neither law nor order; and this distracted existence, which he terms joy and bliss and freedom, continues throughout his life (Jowett 1969).

By emphasizing the aims instead of the forms of government and of learning, classical education combats the tyrannical susceptibilities of democracy. Its whole-embracing dialectic challenges all forms, requiring them to defend themselves in relation to their premises and aims — their first and final causes. In the case of democracy, for instance, one excellent premise for its form is the equality of human souls, although there are others, such as Rousseau's myth of universal human innocence. On the subject of aims, however, classical education is far more explicit. Democracy is a noble form insofar as its aim is to provide the freedom necessary for all people to develop their full human potentials, but it becomes a vile form when, bereft of culture, it abandons this purpose and begins to value freedom for its own sake. When this happens, democracy — which only survives as a means toward higher ends — dies, and the many subtle forms of tyranny begin to infest its rotting corpse.

This leads us to formulate the fourth objective of classical education in democratic society. Because it helps to correct and in some cases to counterbalance the natural excesses and defects of democracy, classical education engages in a perpetual dialectic with society. If school and state are to prosper and to strengthen each other, the school cannot merely reflect democratic society or be an extension of the government's democratizing policies. When the school allows this to happen, a host of tyrannies — individual and social, intellectual and spiritual — begin to erode the freedoms on which democracy is built. The school, therefore, must offer a sort of dialectical negation of democratic society, challenging the policies and attitudes of the state and of society inside the classroom, while educating — paradoxically — aristocrats rather than democrats.

Democracy is a political ideal, not a fact of life. Its infrequent and precarious manifestations have always depended on two types of men, both products of classical education: I refer to the ascendancy of the uncommon man, the Pericles, Lincoln, Roosevelt, or Churchill; and the self-governance of the common man. The uncommon man towers above his contemporaries in ability, wisdom, and virtue, as well as in his commitment to a self-transcending ideal. An awesome sense of responsibility to the past usually haunts him, and he possesses an extraordinary ability to articulate the highest aims of democracy and to persuade his individualistic countrymen to exercise their freedoms in united pursuit of these aims. But more important to the survival of democracy than these uncommon men are the common men whom they govern (or whom they *can* govern) because they are self-governed. To comprehend the rarity of self-governing men, the unshifting ground of greatness, we must examine the education that forms them. What sort of education aims at producing self-governing individuals? To this question, we already know the answer: a normative education that recognizes and brings into balance the domains of the whole person.

But for our present purposes, we might turn this question around and ask: What sort of education fails to produce self-governing individuals? "After the general idea of virtue," writes Alexis de Tocqueville (1956) in his treatise on *Democracy in America*, "I know of no higher principle than that of rights; or rather these two ideas are united in one. The idea of rights is simply that of virtue introduced into the political world." De Tocqueville's comment suggests that an education preoccupied with democratic forms might in its political enthusiasm lay a greater emphasis on rights than on virtue, especially if that education exists as an arm of the state. The accompanying tendency to regard students as social-political animals and to deny the threefold man of classical education will only be exacerbated in a utilitarian era. The virtue of the individual domain and the piety of the religious domain will be subsumed by the political idea of rights.

Ironically, this reductionist feat, performed to prepare the student for democracy by bringing democracy into the classroom, works against the aim of producing self-governing individuals. Whereas virtue and piety extract many obligations from the individual, requiring a significant level of self-mastery and self-sacrifice, the political concept of rights implies a set of obligations owing to the individual. Not only does the democratic-utilitarian education based on rights prevent the student from achieving self-awareness by blotting out two-thirds of his human identity, but it clouds the perception of his relation to others. The student perceives his classmates and fellow citizens as his servants, owing him rights, rather than as his equals to whose rights and needs he owes virtuous and pious submission. Truly, democratic citizens are not born, they are made; and only a classical education with its balanced conception of man and its aristocratic ideal of the life of virtue is apt to form democratic citizens who are more eager to give of their obligations than to receive of their rights.

This is perhaps why the democratic theorist and revolutionary Joseph Mazzini (1966) writes not of man's rights, but of his duties:

> Why do I speak to you of your *duties* before speaking to you of your *rights*? Why is a society in which all, voluntarily or involuntarily, oppress you, in which the exercise of all the rights which belong to man is constantly denied you, in which misery is your lot, and what is called happiness is for other classes of men, why do I speak to you of self-sacrifice and not of conquest; of virtue, moral improvement, education, and not of material *well-being*?

It is in the performance of man's duties to himself, to others, and to God that his rights are important to him. Without a knowledge of these duties, his concept of rights will be selfish and extravagant, tending to enlarge his expectations, while limiting his sense of fulfillment. This rule also applies to education, where the concept of human rights must be derived from the knowledge of man's obligations if the student is to benefit from his democratic liberties by developing his full human potential. Democratic youth does not need his school to tell him what his rights are: they beckon him from every billboard, every television set, and every political soapbox in the land. Nor is the school needed to advise him in securing his rights; indeed, this growing practice may signal the mutual breakdown of democracy and education.

Mazzini fiercely believed that the true source of freedom is the obligatory connection between knowledge and responsibility: man must be free to act on his knowledge. "To be mistaken is a misfortune to be pitied," he writes, "but to know the truth and not to conform one's actions to it is a crime which Heaven and Earth condemn" (Mazzini 1966). A man without the knowledge of the truth — a man ignorant of his obligations to himself, to his neighbors, and to God, and whose education has not aimed at instilling in him a sense of good and evil and a sense of the holy — has no use for rights. He has no knowledge of how to use them, except in a manner that would deny the rights of everyone and everything around him. To insist on such a man's having rights is nothing short of criminal, yet is this not the incredible effect of democracy in the class-room coupled with the utilitarian theories of the modern educator? Surely, when the school fails to instruct man in his duties, the most democratic state in the world is helpless to secure his imagined rights and to satisfy his avaricious longings.

The school, therefore, either strengthens democracy by dialectically challenging the political concept of rights in an effort to produce self-governing people conscious of their manifold duties, or it weakens democracy by basing education on an irresponsible notion of inalienable rights and on an incomplete view of man. Clearly, the object of classical education in a democratic society is to serve the former policy, complementing society's democratic form of government with an aristocratic form of education, while calling into question the aims of the state without unduly honoring its forms. Only in this way will the maintenance of each citizen's privileges be assured by a lively and true sense of his obligations; only in this way will the entire citizen body constitute the sort of norm-minded elite that the logic of democracy demands.

Before leaving this crucial point, we might reconsider it from the standpoint of democracy's natural strengths and weaknesses. No form of government is in practice perfect, and if we want a form of education that will help us perfect our state, we must know what excesses and defects democracy is heir to. Many writers since Thucydides have argued that democracy inherits its weaknesses from its strengths, but few have put their case as succinctly as de Tocqueville (Heffner 1965), who wrote:

> Democracy does not give people the most skilful government, but it produces what the ablest governments are frequently unable to create; namely, an all-pervading and restless activity, a superabundant force, and an energy which is inseparable from it, and which may, however unfavorable circumstances may be, produce wonders. These are the true advantages of democracy.

These "true advantages of democracy" father its excesses, infecting the democratic youth with the distracted existence characterized by Plato and contaminating the state with the aggressive, cocksure, reckless political posture described by Thucydides. The aristocratic form of classical education, however, will direct, shape, and hold in check some of this "all-pervading and restless activity" flowing naturally from democracy. It will bind students to their obligations, hold them responsible for what they know, and ask them to weight their actions and aims against those of its Ideal Type.

If democracy's natural excess is of means, its natural defect is of ends. Whatever a democratic society sets itself to accomplish, as long as the wisdom and perseverance for the task are not lacking, it will with time accomplish it. But real danger lurks in its inability to define meaningful ends, either for itself or for its citizens. When pressed for a definition of ends, it will sometimes prescribe happiness for its citizens and security for itself; but despite an abundance of raw energy trembling to satisfy these imprecise ends, without a universal classical education, democratic society will lack the normative understanding of what choices must be made to secure its clumsy ends or of how to redefine its ends more exactly and meaningfully. Without this normative ability, democracy's explosive energies become more a burden than a blessing to itself, its citizens, and its global neighbors.

Nor will classical education be the natural choice of democracy. The state and the marketplace, looking upon education as a means of ensuring a pliant and productive citizenry, will insist that the school offer a utilitarian education in keeping with their greedy desires; and the democratic youth, with his penchant for restless activity and easy gratification, will prefer self-aggrandizing ends to the self-transcending aims of classical education. But once education surrenders to the will of the state, the marketplace, or the callow youth, democracy's natural affinities will, in de Tocqueville's phrase, "divert the moral and intellectual activity of man to the production of comfort, and the promotion of general well-being." An unruly, ungovernable citizen body, with each person set upon his own comfort and well-being, first at the expense of the state, and then of his neighbor, will unloose destructive forces that can only be held in check temporarily by a system of universal greed. The transcendent aims of education and of democracy having been denied, the two lose their human value and vitality; man, exploiting liberty and learning to fill his belly rather than to find his salvation and to achieve his full human potential, inadvertently throws over his moral democracy for anarchy and tyranny.

The alternative requires holding steadfast to our classical heritage of learning, democracy's utilitarian temptations notwithstanding, and stamping on democratic youth a normative character that inures him to the natural excesses and defects of his society. Democratic youth must be tempered: snatched from the fire of democracy and plunged into the water of classical education. Only this fire-and-water dialectic will prevent the true advantages of democracy from becoming liabilities. For whereas democracy releases the energy enabling man to gain the whole world, he avails himself of this superabundant force, like Faust, at the risk of losing his own soul. It is the prime objective of classical education in a democracy, therefore, to turn man's attention away from worldly gain and onto the soul's salvation. "For what is a man profited, if he shall gain the whole world, and lose his own soul? or what shall a man give in exchange for his soul?"

The well-meaning Mr. Dewey was wrong. Democracy should not try to change the content of a classical education. Instead, it should make normative learning a universal requirement. All men and women, no longer just a small elite, must be taught as if they were the single torchbearers of *paideia*, as if their souls' salvation and civilization's rested upon their stewardship. To the extent that any society fails to provide a rigorous, normative education for all, it creates a social, cultural, and political need for elites. Consequently, it is not those who argue for universal classical education who are elitists, but those who dismiss this view in the name of utility and of democracy.

8

THE PROMISE OF CHRISTIAN PAIDEIA

*If Aristotle, who was a pagan and a philosopher too,
painted such a picture among men who were not holy
and learned in the Scriptures, how much more is it fit for
one who moves in the place of Christ to fulfill the task?*

—Erasmus

I

Why should the student seek to perfect himself? Why should the student stand aside from himself and be always at work chiseling his own statue? How can a refinement of intelligence and sensibility save his soul? How can perfecting the self lead to self-transcendence? Ultimately, the pagan humanism of classical education could not answer these questions. The Stoics' adulation of simplicity, hardship, and self-denial may have hardened man for the ordeal of life, helping him to partake in some measure of the Ideal Type or to die as he had lived, with grace and equanimity, but it never satisfied the craving for a transcendent justification of his absolute standard: that the life of virtue is right despite the hardships of the way and the contrary opinion of many. Consequently, the best of lives often ended — like Cato the Younger's at Utica — in a wistful, meaningless suicide.

Without a transcendent justification, the pagan humanism of the ancient school suffered from three self-destructive diseases. The first was its tendency to push man into the position of supreme value. Although this tendency saved man from becoming the means of accomplishing merely ideological or technological ends, it also encouraged a refined egocentrism, which failed to satisfy man's deepest longings to belong, to transcend his disconcerting self-centeredness, to serve the whole, and to know his purposes and meaning within the context of the whole. The ancient school saved man from becoming an automaton, but at the cost of his transcendent self-awareness, for it taught him to seek inner perfection through a style so refined and self-conscious that in the end, he often became effete and lost the perspective and balance that he had set out to achieve. Juvenal, satirizing the itinerant Greek philosophers of his day, attributes this disease to them.

Second, pagan humanism suffered from a natural tendency toward elitism. This ailment besets all programs for self-improvement and personal salvation that depend entirely upon the talents and efforts of the individual for their success. In ancient times, for instance, the life of virtue excluded women and slaves. The demands of the Ideal Type were such that they enforced a social, economic, political, sexual, and intellectual elitism — and thereby withheld from an overwhelming majority of persons the opportunity to realize a rich and full humanity.

Third, the pagan humanism founded upon Protagoras' grand proclamation that "man is the measure of all things" sowed the contagion of ideological thinking. Despite its scientific tone and its habit of ridiculing the solipsism of former ages, modern ideology grows out of man's desire to furnish himself with a naturalistic explanation for first and final causes and to judge natural and human history against his present needs and perceptions. Evolutionism seats man on the throne of nature and regards all other species of life and sublife as somehow unfulfilled homo sapiens waiting at stages of development through which man has already passed. This permits man to look on the past with the same smug condescension that he lavishes on dinosaurs. Meanwhile, Marxism measures history against man's progressive social development, predicting a synthetic Communist state to round out the ages and stop the whirling carousel of class struggle. (Ironically, to achieve this perfect state, in a perversion of its classical antecedents, the socialist state must educate its citizenry for collective efficiency rather than for the individual development of its full human potential.) In any case, the ideological tendency in pagan humanism finds its ultimate expression in the modern superman, the archetypal monster, who, regarding himself as the supreme end of natural and human history, judges the past but is not judged by it. The superman is deified in the modern ideological state, as he was in ancient Rome, in the person of the ruler. Lenin and Mao succeeded Julius and Augustus.

Modern classical education, however, need not slip into the quicksands of egocentrism, elitism, or ideology, since it is (or ought to be) grounded on a dialectic between pagan humanism and Christianity. This dialectic undergirds all Western thought, culture, and education; in a word, it is the groundwork of *paideia.* To ignore this dialectic in our schools not only introduces error into our calculations about the past and about ourselves, but throws away man's best hope for learning about himself, about his purposes in living, and about the values necessary for accomplishing his purposes. The creative tension between pagan humanism and Christianity animates normative education and promises to lift the student to a level of understanding above reason in an experience of faith. Faith satisfies man's craving for a transcendent justification of the Ideal

Type, at the same time as it makes possible on a universal scale the self-transcendence that the ancient philosophers sought only by esoteric means.

The story of Christ eventually led millions to the experience of faith. This experience made an immediate and enduring impression upon the thoughts and actions of the believer. For the educated believer, the Christian story reconciled the warring camps of pagan philosophy and mythology. Christ embodied the rational principle (the *logos*) in story form (the *mythos*). The Master's reasoning avoided the platitudes and cultural prejudices of most philosophies. His monumental riddles and concerns seemed to come from another world, and he seemed to enlarge the core of Judaic belief, while rejecting its cultural accretions. The story of his life, like all true myths, had a point and a goal. It also presented a picture of truth, not a pattern of truth reducible to a number of generalizations; this picture portrayed a view of man that was complete and comprehensive in a way that no single myth or philosophy ever had been. It was inevitable that the influence of this amazing reconciliation be reflected in the *paideia* of those who shared the experience of faith. My purpose is not, however, to ask why the story of Christ possessed the power to induce belief. The fact that it did is alone important to my argument, for it obliges me to raise the question that this chapter seeks in broad outline to answer: What influence upon *paideia*, specifically upon the development of classical education, did the experience of Christian belief have?

II

Pagan humanism and Christianity agreed that the fundamental problem with man, as well as the greatest obstacle to his learning about himself and his purposes, is his self-centeredness. Man cannot be virtuous or wise until he gets off center. Ancient education, aware of the egocentric dangers lurking in its program of self-polishing, relied heavily on the development of style and conscience to move the student off dead center. Through the study of language and myth, it placed before the student the model of a self-transcending Ideal, while developing in him an "aristocratic" conscience: a conscience that tied the student's rights to duties of self-sacrifice and self-effacement. The conscience, once identified dialectically with the whole of knowledge, challenged man's selfish assumptions and rationalizations and urged him to act on his knowledge of the nonself whole. But conscience could only prod him to search for the means of escaping from the center of his circle. It could not empower him with the means for doing so.

Greek philosophy stepped in, on the one hand, to aid him in this escape with the tools of reason. Like the Canadian novelist Robertson Davies, the philosopher thought he saw in conscience a sort of divine spark, "the inner struggle toward self-knowledge and self-recognition." He hoped by using reason to elicit this spark from his students. It was a bold endeavor, but how exactly self-recognition would lead to self-transcendence was ultimately unclear. One recalls the question attributed to Jowett on his first meeting the poet Rossetti in London: "And tell me, Mr. Rossetti, what were they going to do with the Holy Grail when they found it?" One suspects that many students of philosophy, like the Arthurian knights, found the quest for self-transcendence on paths of self-recognition a rather self-aggrandizing one.

Greek rhetoric, on the other hand, tried to liberate man from his self-centeredness by conforming him to the moral categories of literature. Whereas the philosopher sought to facilitate the natural, dialectical process of intellectual development in the student, the rhetorician emphasized the character-building influence of the content of learning. Skeptical of an elicited spark of self-recognition, he regarded education as a matter of shaping the self (*morphosis*) to conform to the mold of the self-transcending Ideal embodied in great literature. His attitude made the content and style of what the student studied all-important. Admittedly, by confronting the student at an early age with models of self-sacrifice to emulate and examples of self-indulgence to shun, he represented a more prosaic solution than the philosopher to the problem of overcoming man's inveterate self-centeredness.

Although it decidedly favored the rhetoricians, ancient education never resolved the conflict between those who optimistically approached learning as the dialectical development of human personality and those who, with perhaps a lower opinion of human nature, took only into account the influence of the object of learning on the student. Yet at their moments of finest flowering, both ancient schools anticipated the resolution of their conflict in Christianity. Both recognized the need for a positive force empowering man to meet the self-transcendent demands of a conscience that is perpetually negating his self-centeredness, and both identified this positive force complementing the conscience as love — the *eros* of Plato's *Symposium*.

Eros, not to be confused with the predictably self-centered, technique-ridden erotica of our utilitarian era, is the basis for moral action. It entails, repeating Shelley (Baker 1951), "a going out of our own nature, and an identification of ourselves with the beautiful which exists in thought, action, or person, not our own." Love is the principle of truth in philosophy and of beauty in art that draws the spirit of man off center to participate imaginatively in the object of beauty or truth. Love provides man with the means for answering the mandates of conscience and for breaking out of his egocentric prison. Unlike self-denial or self-negation, love is a positive force, but it requires an object above the self for which the self is transcended. Once the knowledge of this transcendent object is established, whether by reason, by example, or by faith, love binds a person to this object. This binding is the supreme aim of classical education, the union of knowledge and responsibility tantamount to the formation of the virtuous man; but without *eros*, even the best pedagogy is helpless to achieve this aim.

Although the ancients recognized the self-transcendent potential of *eros* in human affairs, they were more likely to identify *eros* with the arts because of art's apparent ability to extinguish man's self-centeredness. Art offered the ideal object that love requires, while working at various levels to woo man out of his own nature. First, art at the level of content presented the image of a simple ideal for human form, thought, and action. The art-lover who deliberately sought to model his life after this ideal achieved a measure of self-transcendence, so long as his love for the art's ideal image inspired his thought and action. Second, at the conceptual level, classical art, with its emphasis on ideal forms, provided an experience of the immanent realities otherwise beyond reach of the art-lover's five senses. The perfection of art, like that of geometry, afforded a palpable proof, if one were needed, of man's ability to free himself conceptually from his sensual incarceration. Art at this level permitted the art-lover a direct, if abstract, experience of the transcendent realms.

Finally, at a level sometimes referred to as *anagogic*, art availed man of an opportunity to obliterate the lumpen consciousness of the self in an ecstasy of contemplation or creation. By participating imaginatively in the art, the art-lover seemed, at least for a time, to escape the self and to assuage his raging conscience. The ecstasy of contemplation or creation, the supreme moment of *eros*, purged the conscience by temporarily removing the art-lover from the realms of moral endeavor and planting him in the amoral world of the art-object. The Hellenistic preoccupation with style and with the rules of style perhaps contributed to this effect by repressing the essential element of moral endeavor in all great art. Michaelangelo, as he advanced in years and in creative power, fought off the intoxicating effects of a merely beautiful style, hating his "divine objects" when they afforded him only an ecstatic escape from conscience, but adoring them when they inspired within him a devotion to God, empowering him to live rightly, yes, righteously.

In fact, the ancients' identification of *eros* with art and of creativity with salvation from self-centeredness simply led them back into a humanistic obsession with the self. Art had aided religion by helping man escape from the seering demands of the conscience; it had also served education by showing him how to satisfy his conscience's demands. But the transcendent reality of art that made all this possible was, barring divine revelation, the conceptual creation of man: at best, it was man's intimation of a world in which he could flee the self and quiet the conscience. By confusing his conception of a perfect triangle and his creation of an ideal image with a world in which self-transcendence is possible, the pagan humanist had manufactured a man-made heaven, where art acted as a narcotic momentarily suppressing the demands of conscience. Because this heaven was grounded in the desire of the self, not in the will of God, the pagan humanist's identification of *eros* with the ideal in art short-circuited the transcendent power of love, cultivating a plant that eventually bore fruit in narcissism rather than in self-transcendence.

III

If not through art, how does love empower man to resolve the ancient contradiction between man's desire to know and perfect the self and his desire to
transcend the self? As the early Christian thinkers within the classical tradition
excitedly realized, the answer was provided in the person of Christ: the spirit of
eros incarnate, the expressor of the divine will, and the truly divine object that
self-transcending love requires. Suddenly, there were divine imperatives for all
the fundamental questions about classical education that pagan humanism found
difficult to answer. Why should the student seek to perfect himself? It was the
will of God that all men should model themselves after the person of Christ, the
perfect work of art, God painted in the flesh. The love of this work of art,
because it was incontestably both perfect and transcendent, empowered man to
satisfy the demands of conscience, while relieving him through grace of the
anxiety of conscience.

On the brink of realizing the Christian fulfillment of the pagan philosopher's
intimations and contradictions, early Christian thinkers ignored the rhetorical
nature of Tertullian's question — "What has Athens to do with Jerusalem, what
the Academy with the Church?" — and set about answering him in earnest,
filling libraries with their volumes on a Christian doctrine that seemed at last to
resolve the disturbing questions phrased by Socrates and pondered by every
great mind in the pagan humanist tradition. It is difficult to believe that their
enthusiasm in adapting this tradition to Christian ends was — as the noteworthy
classicist Peter Green maintains — merely a missionary expedient "to beat the
pagan free-thinkers on their own ground and with their own weapons." Even
Saint Paul, who recognized the profound cleavage between pagan humanism and
Christianity, pressed this difference throughout his letters to the fledgling
churches, believing that at the higher level of faith the contradictions of classical
paideia would dissolve, as they had for him, into a transcendent unity of opposites:

> For the Jews require a sign, and the Greeks seek after wisdom: but we
> preach Christ crucified, unto the Jews a stumblingblock, and unto the
> Greeks foolishness; but unto them which are called, both Jews and
> Greeks, Christ the power of God, and the wisdom of God. [From the
> *New Testament*, King James Version]

Christianity resolved contradictions within worldwide Greek *paideia* in some
highly original ways. Christian doctrine, for example, united the philosophical
and rhetorical traditions' contradictory assumptions about the nature of man.
To the question — Is man basically good or bad? — Christian doctrine's answer
allows for the innate conscience and divine spark of the philosopher. The law
written in men's hearts bearing witness to the truth, according to Saint Paul,
is the happy result of man's having been created in the image of God. There is
a Christian as well as a Socratic sense, therefore, in which the knowledge of the
truth comes out of man's self-awareness, elicited by the divine *Logos*. But at the

same time, the Christian doctrine of sin takes into account the rhetorician's low opinion of recalcitrant man.

Even the doctrine of sin makes sense only in relation to man's innate knowledge of the truth. Sin is a condition for which man is responsible as a result of failing to act in accordance with what he knows. Man is culpable in the eyes of God and of his fellows not because he is fundamentally bad, but because he refuses to live as the good law written into his nature tells him he ought to live. Despite the uncompromising warnings of his conscience, he feasts on the fruits of his self-centeredness: pride, greed, hatred, jealousy, stupidity, and fear. That man is responsible for his knowledge of the truth, even the knowledge over which he has no control and from which he tries to hide, is not an idea invented by the early Christian thinkers. It constitutes the Greek insight into the nature of tragedy. But between Greek tragedy and Christian sin there is one major difference: tragedy is inescapable and therefore somehow ennobling, but sin is neither.

Although the ancients saw man's fate as tied up with his character and tried through education to mold character with philosophical reason and rhetorical example, they also recognized the futility of seeking to avert life's inevitable tragedy. Surrounding the ancients' efforts to resolve the contradiction between good and evil in man, there was a quality of fatalism, of ultimate resignation, that more than anything else perhaps caused their unwillingness to turn science into an instrument for relieving human suffering. Basically, they were pessimistic about life and the possibility of finally knowing or realizing its purposes. In the end, they were not convinced that reason and example are sufficient to make the connection between knowledge and responsibility, causing man to act in perfect harmony with what he knows.

Up to a point, early Christians shared the ancients' pessimism. They despaired of the power of reason or example to force the conversion, the inner change, the *morphosis*, the development of personality that a satisfactory resolution of the contradiction between good and evil in man demands. They too doubted that a connection between knowledge and responsibility comes about naturally, as simplistic analogies between the development of personality and the growth of the physical body imply. The spiritual process called *education* is not spontaneous in nature, but requires constant care.

But setting aside these reservations, they viewed the problem hopefully. For knowledge, the Christians believed, can since the advent of Christ be successfully joined to responsibility at the level of faith. Just as dogma that is put to the test of experience sustains dialectic, so faith grows out of acting upon one's beliefs. "The fear of the Lord is the beginning of wisdom," wrote the Psalmist, "a good understanding have all they that do his commandments." By resolving the contradiction between the good and evil in man at the level of faith, promising a knowledge of life's meaning and purposes happily wedded to man's responsibility, Christianity injected a hopeful note and rewarded the classical tradition's strivings for a link between right thinking and right acting.

IV

By contrast, the modern school has abandoned the classical striving after a normative education, as well as the hopeful Christian *paideia* that crowned the ancient tradition. Instead, it adopts a posture of nondogmatic, value-free learning that is not only false, but dangerous. As Theodore Sizer (1973) in his popular book on the modern school, *Places for Learning, Places for Joy*, writes:

> General expectations notwithstanding, there is no such thing as a value-free school. Schools have to take moral positions just to operate. They have to treat children in one way or another and thus willy-nilly teach a set of norms by example. No teacher exists in a vacuum wholly value-free (how dull he would be!),

and we might interject, how dull his value-free affectation often makes him,

> . . . nor is any teacher conceivably able to argue every side of every issue. He selects and in so doing implies values. The very act of presenting several sides of an issue is itself an expression of value. As for religion, however defined, it is inevitably "taught" in countless classrooms. One cannot discuss history, literature, or the arts, without some consideration of church doctrine and of peoples' religious motivations. Formal religion is on many children's minds; and no good teacher can avoid, eventually, what is on the children's minds.

To this just observation we might add four of our own. First, what is significant is not that the modern school cannot rid itself of values, but that "general expectations" should wish it to do so. Second, what is amazing is not the consideration "of peoples' religious motivations" in "countless classrooms," but the total absence and conscientious avoidance of such considerations in countless more classrooms.

Third, what is worth remarking is not that our schools "inevitably" teach values by implication and by innuendo every day, but that the grounds for these values — whatever they are — are devious and inaccessible because hidden or ignored. Arnold Toynbee (1962), writing about historians who conceal their theological predilections, suggests the unseen danger in this implicit approach to values and to religious dogma:

> In the Jewish-Christian-Muslim *Weltanschauung*, history is set in a framework of theology. This traditional Western vista of history has been rejected by many Western historians — and by their non-Western disciples too — during the last two centuries and a half. Yet I believe that every student of human affairs does have a theology, whether he acknowledges this or not; and I believe that he is most at the mercy of his theology when he is most successful in keeping it repressed below the threshold of his consciousness.

From the teacher's point of view, then, education will be freer of unexamined, problematical presuppositions when he faces the normative implications of his task squarely. From the student's standpoint, education will be — shall we say — less subversive when his teacher possesses a forthright and articulate sense of values, rather than when his teacher has values that he has chosen to conceal or of which he is unaware.

Fourth, what really matters is not so much what is taught (although the normative character of great literature is emphatically preferred), but how it is taught. To teach art and letters analytically, holding the question of value by the throat at arm's length, is to wrest life from learning and to promote the illusion of knowledge without responsibility. This analytical distortion of our artistic and literary inheritance fulfills the pagan definition of tragedy and depicts the Christian doctrine of Fallen Man. Since the Nazi atrocities of this century and the horror of hearing Mozart at Auschwitz, many have ridiculed Cicero's belief in the moral efficacy of teaching the humane letters, but few have stopped to consider how that generation of Germans learned their letters. Indeed, their gymnasiums — not the cloyingly upright English public schools we are so fond of satirizing — were the forerunners of our own highly analytical and utilitarian academies.

Can we humanize the young by giving them a humanistic education? Can a child memorize endless passages of Shakespeare or Goethe and still turn out to be a beast? The answer to both questions is yes, because the intention of the learner, not the content of his lessons, is alone critical to the moral efficacy of education. The learner must want to be changed by his studies. He must read Shakespeare as a Christian reads his Bible. "Whenever the prince picks up a book," advised Erasmus (1965), "he should do so not with the idea of gaining pleasure but of bettering himself by his reading. He who really wants to be better can easily find the means of becoming better. A great part of goodness is the desire to be good." The greatest part of education is instilling in the young the desire to be good: a desire that sharpens and shapes their understanding, that motivates and sustains their curiosity, and that imbues their studies with transcendent value. To the pagan dictum that virtue is the fruit of learning, the Christian added, "And learning is the fruit of virtue," thereby interjecting a mystical element into the already complex relation between knowledge and responsibility.

Purged of pagan complexity and Christian mystery, modern education's habit of considering everything analytically as a physical datum fails to inspire change in the learner. Philosophy, religion, history, literature — all become mere physical data. This posture of analytical, value-free learning diametrically opposes the wisdom of both pagan and Christian *paideia*. It methodically strips our cultural inheritance in the arts and letters of its normative richness and encourages modern youth in the deadly presumption of amoral action. The way a modern youth learns does not admit, let alone emphasize, the connection between knowledge and responsibility. Yet to paraphrase Bacon in a context he now deserves: to give a man knowledge is to give him a sword. To teach man the devastating science of swordsmanship and not the moral implications and responsibilities that come with wielding a sword is to unloose upon the world both a murderer and a victim. This is a tragedy in both instances, since modern man's eleventh-hour plea of ignorance in regard to his responsibilities will be — despite his vast stores of piecemeal knowledge — quite useless to save him.

V

By establishing the identity of the *Eros* and by insisting on the faith-connection between knowledge and responsibility, Christian *paideia* fulfilled the promise of classical education by avoiding the egocentric and ideological pitfalls of pagan humanism. For the Christian, God in Christ firmly occupied the position of supreme value: this fact became the cornerstone of responsible learning and saved the conscience from being at odds with the self. So long as classical education remained centered in the self, even if just for the purpose of transcending the self, conscience rebelled. But this contradiction between the self-seeking perfection and the conscience desiring transcendence was relieved by Christian *paideia*, wherein Christ replaced self and the demands of conscience were met. "The *paideia* of the Christian is *imitatio Christi*: Christ must take shape in him," writes Werner Jaeger (1961) in *Greek Paideia and Early Christianity*. The influential object of learning became the incarnate God rather than an abstract, humanist Ideal Type, and the incompleteness of the pagan tradition was rendered whole by the Christian ideal.

As Cicero expected the Ideal Type to take shape in the student through his study of Greek literature, so Gregory of Nyssa (Jaeger 1961) regarded the formation of Christ in the Christian as the effect of his biblical studies.

> Literature is *paideia*, in so far as it contains the highest norms of human life, which in it have taken on their lasting and most impressive form. It is the ideal picture of man, the great paradigm. Gregory clearly sees the analogy between this Greek concept of literature and the function of the Bible. He did not read the Bible as literature, as the modern tendency is. That would be a complete misunderstanding of his concept of literature, which was the Greek concept of literature as *paideia*.

Throughout his book, Jaeger underlines the formative function of literature in the classical tradition. Christian *paideia* inherited and strengthened this concept of literature. Neither the philological fact of what is written nor the meaning of what is written signifies the *paideia* of the classical and Christian texts. Literature as *paideia* is studied to call forth an inner change, the *morphosis*, the transformation of life, and the formation of virtue that is the highest end of education. The old meaning of *paideia* as it is used in the Septuagint, still clings to the word: " . . . the chastisement of the sinner that brings about a change of mind in him" (Jaeger 1961). Literature as *paideia* does not necessarily change the fact or meaning of what is written, but it does alter the spirit in which the student pursues his studies and shapes the questions with which he confronts his reading. These questions are what we have called *normative* — and analysis serves them, not itself.

Christian *paideia* differed from pagan *paideia*, however, because a principle of holiness rather than of perfection directed the formative function of normative inquiry. Christian holiness elevates the significance of everything, recognizing in even a sparrow or a mustard seed the object of divine compassion; but according to pagan humanism, everything derives its significance from its relation and usefulness to man. Christian holiness acknowledges that knowledge and power are attributes of God. The man who assumes for himself knowledge and power finds only ignorance and corruption. This was Adam's presumption and the cause of man's fall; its antithesis in Christ's response to his Father — "not my will but thine be done" — was the New Adam's glory and the cause of man's salvation. Whereas through Adam's presumption, error entered the world, through Christ's holy example, error is corrected in the experience of faith. Hence, the ideal of Christian holiness emphasizes the action of God in the life of the individual, making worthiness contingent on the will and work of God, as well as on the free choice and participation of man; but pagan humanism's ideal of perfection blurs the distinction between human and divine wills, fostering a subtly egoistic attitude in the student that either intensifies his self-centeredness or aggravates his conscience. Christian holiness heals this breach between the self and the conscience with the balm of selfless love. The holy man loves an object not because of its usefulness or attractiveness to him, but — *imitatio Christi* — because of God's love for it. Christian *paideia*, therefore, urges man to aspire to be holy by loving above self the Creator and His creation, rather than to become trapped in the ancient contradiction between self and conscience, seeking through love of self an insular and esoteric perfection. In theory, at least, this is how Christian *paideia* subverted the egocentric tendencies of pagan humanism, while also hardening man against the ideological temptation to read his own selfish purposes into natural and human history.

VI

In the third century of the Christian era, the pagan philosopher Plotinus (Schumacher 1977) wrote that "knowing demands the organ fitted to the object." Whereas the five senses are sufficient to know the material object, the ancients held that a higher organ must be cultivated or implanted if man is to possess a knowledge of God's purposes, of man's best choice of ends, and of life's complete happiness. Aristotle (1975) called this higher organ, or divine element, the "intellect." "What we have to do," he said, "is to put on immortality so far as we may, and to do all that we do with the view of living the life of the highest thing in us." Although the higher organ was often associated with the mind, especially among the Greeks, its function was not always synonymous with reason. Despite his careful elaboration of a dialectical process for arriving at the true, the good, and the beautiful, Socrates invariably attended to the inner voice of his numinous *daimon*, even when doing so seemed to hinder the logic of his argument. Beginning with Homer and extending throughout the entire corpus of Greek literature, one finds allusions to the needful presence of divine assistance in the human quest for understanding.

The modern, with his arsenal of scientific theory and methodology, is apt to find these recurring allusions a nuisance and to dismiss them as mumbo jumbo, poetic devices, atavistic superstitions — in the case of the great philosopher, some dangling superfluity of his evolving consciousness. But the Christian, with perhaps less prejudice, recognized that one's openness to divine assistance is not a matter of intelligence, of science, or of evolution, but of faith. The modern who chooses to exclude all nonphysical organs from his quest for understanding drastically limits the objects of his search. His belief only in matter confines his sight only to matter. It is as if with the invention of the Geiger counter, man had arbitrarily decided to exclude everything but radioactive substances from his field of inquiry, protesting that he could neither prove the existence nor gain knowledge of what failed to register on his new machine. "The result is not factual error," as Schumacher (1977) points out, "but something much more serious: an inadequate and impoverished view of reality."

Saint Paul in his first letter to the Corinthian church explained a paideutic law that was not novel to his educated Greek readers:

> But as it is written, Eye hath not seen, nor ear heard, neither have entered into the heart of man, the things which God hath prepared for them that love him. But God hath revealed them unto us by his Spirit: for the Spirit searcheth all things, yea, the deep things of God. For what man knoweth the things of a man, save the spirit of man which is in him? even so the things of God knoweth no man, but the Spirit of God.

According to Saint Paul, Christian *paideia* realized the transcendent objectives of classical education by offering access to the source of truth through prayer and access to the spiritual reality underlying the material universe through the indwelling Spirit of God: "But the natural man receiveth not the things of the Spirit of God: for they are foolishness unto him: neither can he know them, because they are spiritually discerned." Christ himself characterized the condition of men who refuse this divine assistance, the "natural man" (*psuchikos*) of Saint Paul's passage, as: "They, seeing, see not; and hearing they hear not, neither do they understand." At this point, the Christian doctrine of divine grace rescued the pagan from his unfulfilled longing for a higher organ adequate to know the answers to his perplexing normative questions. For whether he conceived of grace as the joint effort of man and the Spirit of God or as the unique work of the Spirit, the Christian acknowledged the essential power of his faith to enlarge his understanding of the world and of his meaning and purposes in it.

Far from opposing them, this attribute of the Christian revelation accomplished the goals of classical education — a fact that undoubtedly promoted the gradual and widespread acceptance of the new faith. Nor was the significance of this spiritual dimension in education doubted by either pagan or Christian until the modern era, when science, "on account of its methodical restriction and its systematic disregard of higher levels," drew the conclusion already conspicuously lodged in its assumptions, namely, that there is no palpable evidence of the existence of any such higher levels, or of the corresponding higher organs in the individual. In this ideological straightjacket, Schumacher (1977) argues that "faith, instead of being taken as a guide leading the intellect to an understanding of the higher levels, is seen as opposing and rejecting the intellect and is therefore itself rejected."

VII

Above all, as has been twice touched upon already, Christian *paideia* crowned the education of antiquity by repudiating the distinction between knowing the truth and doing the good. This repudiation, thanks to Plato and Isokrates, already existed in the waning philosophical and rhetorical traditions of the ancients. With their pedagogical emphasis on forming the virtuous man, using the literary mold of the Ideal Type (the *paideia*) to shape the young scholar (the *morphosis*), they had struggled to unite the intellect and the will; but at best, they had achieved only fleeting and isolated successes. It remained for the Christian writers of the apostolic era to resolve this crucial contradiction between knowing and doing with their message of faith and love.

Perhaps because of his rigorous schooling in Greek philosophy, Saint Paul's discovery of the unity of intellect and will in the life of faith made the theme almost an obsession with him in his preaching. His writings disclose an impatience with the proverbial ecclesiastical controversy between faith and works, in which faith is regarded as the knowledge of God and works as the doing of His will. In fact, Saint Paul taught that faith embraces both knowing and doing through the power of Christ. Thus, on Mars Hill, in his brilliant appeal to the Greeks, the Apostle united the great opposites of intellect and will in Christ "in whom we live, and move, and have our being." Faith succeeded through the power of Christ where the Ideal Type of pagan humanism failed to raise man from his fallen state and to avert the tragic consequences of knowledge without responsibility. Christ embodied for the Christian a new Ideal Type — with traces of the old, but no longer rooted in the social order or reducible to a set of ethical platitudes. Although Christ as Ideal Type continued to be the object of dialectical learning, he was not subject to inclusion in a pantheon of ideal predecessors. He entered time only briefly to complete and perfect the tyrannizing image.

After him, there would be no more myths of heroes adding their idiosyncracies to the evolving shape of the Ideal Type. The myths of heroes would give way to the lives of saints, men and women who partook of the Ideal Type but did not presume to enlarge upon it. In their lives, knowledge would joyously court responsibility and intellect would wed the will. This is why Saint James wrote: "Even so faith, if it hath not works, is dead, being alone." The idea without the deed simply demonstrates an absence of faith — no sainthood in that.

Centuries after Saint Paul, Erasmus (1965), in his advice to a Christian prince, equated the active life with the philosophical life, citing supporting evidence from Book VI of Plato's *Republic*:

> I do not mean by philosopher, one who is learned in the ways of dialectic or physics, but one who casts aside the false pseudo-realities and with open mind seeks and follows the truth. To be a philosopher and to be a Christian is synonymous in fact. The only difference is in the nomenclature.

The *paideia* of Erasmus, being devoutly Christian, made no distinction between seeking and following the truth: in a life surrendered to the claims of faith and love, the one included the other. At last, the theoretic life of Aristotle, the life of virtue, transcended the philosopher's political prerequisites and realized its universal promise in the life of faith.

VIII

Athens on the day that Saint Paul encountered the altar to the unknown god presents a peculiarly contemporary scene. First, dialectic in the Academy is dead. Serious dialogue over the most important questions affecting man during his brief sojourn on earth is missing. No one any longer asks: What is the purpose and meaning of human existence? What are man's absolute rights and duties? What is good, and what is evil? What is morality if every quality of life is reduced to what is convenient or to what brings the greatest pleasure? What is truth if all knowledge derives from the scientific analysis of physical data? In short, the interest in learning is essentially trivial. ("For all the Athenians and strangers which were there spent their time in nothing else, but either to tell, or to hear some new thing.")

Second, Athens is the city of a spiritually illiterate yet god-fearing people. Saint Paul finds the Athenians, amidst a great hubbub of learning, petty in their academic pursuits and superstitious in their religious beliefs. The shades of Plato and Isokrates must have looked upon their intellectual offspring with shamed faces. The high normative purposes of learning had sunk to the mean desire "to hear some new things"; education had lost its transcendent value, its spiritual dimension, and the power of *morphosis* vital to *paideia*. But to the few who ran after the Apostle and believed, the Gospel of Christ must have seemed the very apotheosis of their languishing pagan *paideia* and the sure foundation for a nobler and more effective *paideia*.

My reason for concluding this discussion of the idea of a classical education with the promise of Christian *paideia* is not to convert my reader, but to convince him of the profound and thoughtful integration of the classical and Christian traditions, which the modern school — with an alarming smugness — jettisons. Yet I believe that the dialectic between pagan humanism and Christianity must be revived in the classroom if education in the United States is going to fulfill its paideutic obligations toward the young. Although pagan humanism and modern utilitarianism permit an elitist form of *paideia*, Christianity alone supports our democratic appeal for universal classical education by ascribing a transcendent value to learning. Normative education is both a universal human need and a divine imperative, because the value of *paideia* to the person of faith, whether Christian or Jew, is not merely social or political, but intensely personal and religious as well. For the individual who lives enthusiastically in all his human domains, the modern school's neglect of normative learning and its complacency with regard to either Aristotle's life of virtue or Saint Paul's life of faith are infuriating, because they pull *paideia* up by the roots and leave it to wither in the scorching sun of analysis. Consequently, our young people leave school somewhat confident and somewhat haughty in the means they possess, but incapable of knowing and following their human destiny wisely and virtuously.

There is no benediction in their leave taking, no majestic affirmation of the synthesis between *paideia* and faith, nothing resembling Saint Paul's parting words to the young church at Philippi:

> And now, my friends, all that is true, all that is noble, all that is just and pure, all that is lovable and gracious, whatever is excellent and admirable — fill all your thoughts with these things. The lessons I have taught you, the tradition I have passed on, all that you heard me say or saw me do, put into practice; and the God of peace will be with you.

PART II

THE PRACTICE OF
A CLASSICAL EDUCATION

9

A CURRICULUM PROPOSAL
(WHAT MIGHT HAVE BEEN)

*A classical culture can be defined as a unified collection
of great masterpieces existing as the recognized basis of
its scale of values.*

−*H. I. Marrou*

I

It has been said that a man with an experience is never at the mercy of a man
with an argument. For this reason, it may seem strange that I have chosen to
turn the long experience of classical education into an argument. But in fact,
over two thousand years of classical education has been vanquished by an argument, and those who made this argument are now, in effect, running our schools.
As critics of classical education, these social scientists made some salutary
observations, but as guardians of the educational enterprise, they are a disaster.
Because as theorists, they use statistics rather than logic or authoritative texts
to defend their theories, they come off as having all the answers, or what is
worse, as having discovered all the answers. This arrogance, for that is what it is
no matter how sweetly and cautiously the answers are intoned, blinds them to
two ruinous facts about their methods. First, their methods exclude vast realms
of human knowledge and experience from the inquiry, and second, their
methods make no distinction between statistics that are significant and those
that are merely correct. Consequently, the modern educator tends to define his
tasks too narrowly, and when things go wrong, his impulse is to double-check
his calculations rather than to doubt the significance of his research. He finds
it impossible to understand that a correct answer can be a wrong answer.

Government and its money encourage him in this delusion by creating the
need for "objective criteria." These criteria do not and cannot measure quality,
or for that matter many of the goals they propose to measure; nevertheless,

they strongly suggest a correlation between statistical correctness and significance. Combined with the positivist methods of social science, the pragmatic concerns of government cause attention to be turned to measureable issues, worthy as they may be, like bussing and lunch programs, even though these have nothing to do with what is happening between the teacher and the student.

Nowhere is this confusion of quality and quantity so evident as in the area of teacher certification. All states require a growing number of so-called education courses that teachers must complete in order to teach. It matters not that many of these courses are redundant, irrelevant, mundane, or boring. Although many professional educators admit that these requirements cannot produce effective teachers and that effective teachers generally do not need these courses, there is no move to reduce these quantitative measures or to replace them with qualitative ones. Why not? Perhaps for many of the same reasons that the courtesans who served the temple of Diana in Ephesus resisted Christianity. It not only stripped away the security of their superstitious beliefs, but also threatened their livelihood. Similarly, the educational establishment clings to the superstitious belief in quantity. It assumes that more tax dollars will create better schools, that more educational course requirements will make better teachers, and that more social research will uncover better teaching aims and methods. None of these assumptions is validated, however, by the same establishment's measurements of the declining "quality" of our schools and, by inference, of our teachers' aims and methods.

If, therefore, I have turned the rich experience of classical education into a poor argument, it has been to plead the case against the modern school, while asking my reader, who, like myself, is at least to some extent a product of that school, to consider the oldest and noblest task of education: what I have called *normative learning.* It must be with a deepening sense of frustration and despair that the custodians of *paideia* have watched the decay of normative learning in private and state education since World War II. To be sure, there has been no lack of shiny new school buildings, each offering a smorgasbord of new courses to rival its own hot-lunch program. But the quality of learning cannot be measured in terms of school construction costs and new federal programs. What happens is not necessarily what ought to happen, and the feasibility study — because it generally takes so little into account — seldom indicates what is truly possible. Looking over the centuries-old progress of classical education, one must imagine what might have been, and one must ask what education in the United States today ought to be.

After World War II, it seemed economically feasible — perhaps for the first time in human history — to offer the blessings of *paideia* to more than just an elite of well-born or intellectually gifted young people. But at the very moment when this dream seemed within reach of the overwhelming majority of Americans, education left the path of normative learning to chase after two elusive political objectives: plenty and equality. At first, plenty was assumed to guarantee equality. The war had demonstrated the capability of U.S. industry, when supplied with trained men and women, to produce plenty for all. American industry's victory over two formidable enemies, Germany and Japan, as well as over the Great Depression, bred in many Americans the illusion that there was no problem a prosperous economy could not solve. The sheer superabundance of goods, Americans believed, would overwhelm whatever nagging problems of inequality lay in the background — and what they meant by inequality was, characteristically, poverty: an unequal share of the wealth. Education, therefore, was assigned the task of training men and women to produce plenty for all, so that no one's share of the wealth would be so small that he would have to go without.

As Plato, Thucydides, and de Tocqueville have all observed, democracies prefer to look for material solutions to their spiritual problems. They never despair of making up the difference between the citizen's desires and personal fulfillment with greater production or with a more equitable distribution of goods. Indeed, this is the reason for democracy's basic optimism. But by the mid-1950s, it became clear that plenty was not solving the problem of inequality. In gross terms, there was of course plenty for all, but it was not reaching a sizable segment of the population. This deprived segment — it was decided in the parlance of the day — lacked an "equal opportunity" to lay hands on its share of the wealth. Again, U.S. society turned to its schools to provide this missing opportunity. But because equal opportunity was viewed in terms of getting ahead or getting a job or "getting mine" and not in terms of giving every person his due to an education that would enable him to reach his fullest human potential, the result was a lowering of academic standards to accommodate the weak, indolent, or unmotivated student and a dismantling of the remaining *paideia* in favor of training for "marketable" skills. Classical education could stay only if it could prove its practical value in the marketplace. It became more important to master a specific process than to understand a general principle, and the content of learning became unimportant, so long as it trained the student to do something that would permit him to earn his share of the wealth and thereby help society solve the problem of inequality.

Putting aside our misgivings as to the sagacity of imposing political objectives on the school, are we not still entitled to ask whether modern education has accomplished its utilitarian goals? Has it significantly added to American plenty and equality? I would argue at the secondary school level: no. Whatever gross additions it has made, they are neither significant in achieving the political objectives nor are they worth the infinite cost of depriving future generations of their rightful and necessary *paideia*. Our plenty — perhaps because we cannot imagine life without it — means nothing to us, while hiding from us the lavishly wasteful and destructive consequences of its production. Meanwhile, we seem farther from equality than ever because we have not learned the truth of Socrates, who found his plenty and equality walking through Athens' overladen *agora*, desiring nothing. Instead, we teach our children to crave much and to respect themselves and others in terms of their wealth — that is, of their vulgar ability to accumulate nonliving matter. We have made education the gateway to riches rather than to contentment.

We have yet to see the final debauch of utilitarian learning. In another decade, its ugly manifestations are likely to be epidemic, as our children's demand for goods and services outruns even their burgeoning technology's ability to satisfy them. Nevertheless, rather than counterattack the market-place's vicious onslaught on the appetites of the young, our schools — by refurbishing their curriculums and philosophies to meet the utilitarian demands of democratic society — add their substantial weight to the attack. Education's so-called progressivism merely toadies to mercenary society, endangering both in the consequent loss of dialectic. Trapped by the logic of their positivist presuppositions, both school and society grasp at material straws in the winds of spiritual dissolution and decay. Yet the harder they try to connect material prosperity and functional efficiency with personal fulfillment and charitable humanity, the worse their general malaise and frustration grow — and the hiatus between desire and fulfillment in each individual and in society as a whole gapes wider.

This conviction, none other, prompts the writing of this book and beckons me to ask: What would the modern school look like if it had not chosen willy-nilly to ignore the needs of the whole man in order to outfit him for political expediency and social utility, if it had not departed from the well-charted high road of classical learning? What is the approximate shape of *paideia* in the modern era? What follows, therefore, is an outline, explanation, and sometimes justification for an admittedly personal answer to these questions. Where this answer fails to appeal and win acceptance, I hope that it provokes a dialectical response. To begin with, then, I offer a sample of the classical curriculum, with a list of suggested readings and a daily schedule to demonstrate its practicality.

II

THE CLASSICAL CURRICULUM (GRADES 7-12)

GRADE 7:
  I. MATHS AND SCIENCES
      A. Pre-algebra (1/9)
      B. Earth Science I (1/9)
  II. ARTS AND LANGUAGES
      A. Fine Arts: projects in music, drawing, painting, architecture, and so forth, keying on the Humane Letters syllabus (1/9)*
      B. Performing Arts: choice of choral music, instrumental music/orchestra, drama, or dance (1/9)*
      C. Latin I, French I, German I, or Spanish I (1/9)

---

*Meets in two-period blocks twice a week.

III. HUMANE LETTERS (3/9)
   A. Outline text: Churchill, *The Birth of Britain*
      The New World, part 1
     T. H. White, *The Once and Future King*
     Sir Gawain and the Green Knight
     Tennyson, *Idylls of the King*, esp. "Morte d'Arthur"
     Twain, *A Connecticut Yankee in King Arthur's Court*

     Bede, excerpts from *A History of the English Church*
     Beowulf (recordings available)
     J. Gardner, *Grendel*
     Keats, "Eve of Saint Agnes"

     Scott, *Ivanhoe*
     Magna Carta
     Shakespeare, *Richard II*
       1 Henry IV

     Anouilh, *Beckett*
     The Gospel According to Saint Luke
     Bolt, *A Man for All Seasons*
     More, *Utopia*
   B. Tolkien, *Lord of the Rings* Trilogy (out-of-class reading project)
   C. By memory:
      (a) Tennyson, "And slowly answered Arthur from the barge,"
         from *Idylls*
      (b) Poe, "Eldorado"
      (c) Keats, "La Belle Dame Sans Merci"
      (d) Shakespeare, "Let's talk of graves, of worms, and epitaphs,"
         from *Richard II*
IV. PHYSICAL EDUCATION (1/9)

GRADE 8:
  I. MATHS AND SCIENCES
    A. Algebra I (1/9)
    B. Earth Science II (1/9)
  II. ARTS AND LANGUAGES
    A. Fine Arts: see Grade 7 (1/9)*
    B. Performing Arts: see Grade 7 (1/9)*
    C. Latin II, French II, etc. (1/9)

---

*Meets in two-period blocks twice a week.

III. HUMANE LETTERS (3/9)
    A. Outline text: Churchill, *The New World*, pts. 2 and 3
        The Age of Revolution
        The Great Democracies

        M. Chute, *Shakespeare of London*
        Shakespeare, *The Tempest*
        Marlowe, *Doctor Faustus*
           "Passionate Shepherd to His Love"
        Raleigh, "The Nymph's Reply to the Shepherd"
        Donne, "The Bait"
           "Go and Catch a Falling Star"
           "Batter My Heart"
           "Death, Be Not Proud"
           "Meditation XVII"

        Bunyan, *The Pilgrim's Progress* (abridged)
        Epistle of Saint James
        Mayflower Compact
        Excerpts from: Jonathan Edwards' sermons, Wollman's and
           Crevecoeur's journals, Benjamin Franklin, and Red Jacket
        Hawthorne, *The Scarlet Letter*
        Jefferson, Declaration of Independence
        Burke, "Speech on Conciliation with the Colonies"
        Dickens, *A Tale of Two Cities*
        Melville, *Billy Budd*
        Crane, *Red Badge of Courage*
        Dickens, *Great Expectations*
    B. Kenneth Roberts (out-of-class reading project)
    C. By memory:
        (a) Shakespeare, "A Sea-Dirge" from *The Tempest*
        (b) Marlowe, "Ah Faustus, Now Hast Thou But One Bare Hour
            To Live"
        (c) Donne, "Batter My Heart"
        (d) Blake, "The Tiger"
        (e) Tennyson, "Charge of the Light Brigade"
        (f) Coleridge, "Kubla Khan"
IV. PHYSICAL EDUCATION (1/9)

GRADE 9:
    I. MATHS AND SCIENCES
        A. Geometry: plane, solid, coordinate (1/9)
        B. Biology (2/9)*

---

*Lab sciences occupy six periods a week, four classes and two laboratories.

II. ARTS AND LANGUAGES
  A. Fine Arts: see Grade 7 (1/9)*
  B. Performing Arts: see Grade 7 (1/9)*
  C. Greek I, Russian I, Latin III, French III, etc. (1/9)
III. HUMANE LETTERS (3/9)
  A. Outline texts: Harrison/Sullivan, *A Short History of Western Civilization*
    Starr, *The Ancient Greeks*
      The Ancient Romans
    Penguin's *Atlas of the Ancient World*
    Ceram, *Gods, Graves and Scholars*

  J. W. Johnson, "Creation" from *God's Trombones*
  Book of Genesis
  Gilgamesh (Herbert Mason ed.)
  First and second books of Samuel

  Byron, "The Destruction of Sennacherib"
  Nash, "Very Like a Whale"

  Primary source readings in mythic prototypes:
    Egyptian, Akkadian, Hebraic, Greek†

  Homer, *The Iliad*
    The Odyssey
  Sophocles, *Oedipus the King*
    Oedipus at Colonus
    Antigone
  Aristotle, *Poetics* (selections)
  C. S. Lewis, *Till We Have Faces*

  Herodotus, *History of the Persian Wars* (abridged)
  Book of Ezra
  Book of Esther
  Book of Nehemiah

  Thucydides, *History of the Peloponnesian Wars*
    (Livingston abridged ed.)
  Plutarch, *Themistocles*
    Pericles
    Alcibiades

---

*Meets in two-period blocks twice a week.

†The five prototypes are: Creation; Origin of Evil; Nature of God; World Destruction (Flood); and Origin of Language and World Disunity (Babel).

Excerpts from Hippocrates
Euclid, *Elements of Geometry*

Plato, *Apology*
    Crito
Aristophanes, *The Clouds*
Plato, *Meno*

Book of Job
MacLeish, *J.B.*
B. Mary Renault (out-of-class reading project)
C. By memory:
    (a) Psalm 8, "What Is Man?"
    (b) Psalm 19, "God's Glory"
    (c) Psalm 23, "Twenty-third Psalm"
    (d) Psalm 137, "A Song of Exile"
    (e) Thucydides, "Fix your eyes on the greatness of Athens" from Pericles' Funeral Oration

GRADE 10:
  I. MATHS AND SCIENCES
     A. Algebra II (1/9)
     B. Chemistry (2/9)*
 II. ARTS AND LANGUAGES
     A. Fine Arts: see Grade 7 (1/9)†
     B. Performing Arts: see Grade 7 (1/9)†
     C. Greek II, Russian II, Latin IV, French IV, etc. (1/9)
III. HUMANE LETTERS (3/9)
     A. Outline texts: Harrison/Sullivan, *A Short History of Western Civilization*
        Dorothy Mills, *The Middle Ages*
        F. H. Littell, *Macmillan Atlas History of Christianity*

     Selections from Livy
     Shakespeare, *Julius Caesar*
     Selections from Tacitus
     Juvenal, *Satires I, III, and X*
     Graves, *I, Claudius*
     Virgil, *The Aeneid* (selections)

     Stott, *Basic Christianity*
     The Gospel According to Saint John

---

*Lab sciences occupy six periods a week, four classes and two laboratories.
†Meets in two-period blocks twice a week.

Eliot, *The Cocktail Party*
Acts of the Apostles
Saint Augustine, *Confessions*
Dante, *The Inferno*

Malory, *Le Morte d'Arthur* (selections)
Song of Roland (Dorothy Sayers ed.)
Cervantes, *Don Quixote* (abridged)
Cellini, *Autobiography* (selections)
Shakespeare, *Merchant of Venice*

Chaucer, *The Canterbury Tales* (selections)
Rabelais, *Gargantua and Pantagruel*, books 1 and 2
Erasmus, *Colloquies* (selections)
Reade, *The Cloister and the Hearth*
Janet Lewis, *The Wife of Martin Guerre*

Pico, "Oration on the Dignity of Man"
Erasmus and Luther, *Discourse on Free Will*
Calvin, *Institutes of the Christian Religion* (selections)

Montaigne, *Essays* (selections)
Machiavelli, *The Prince*
Erasmus, *Education of a Christian Prince* (selections)
Shakespeare, *Hamlet*

Shaw, *Saint Joan*
Eliot, *Murder in the Cathedral*
Pirandello, *Henry IV*
Brecht, *Galileo*

B. The Crusades (research paper project): Discuss the social, political, economic, or cultural impact of the Crusades on Western Europe in 3,000 to 5,000 words. This paper should exhibit a wide reading, as well as an ability to narrow down a large topic and argue a thesis clearly and convincingly. It is submitted to the Grade 10 Teachers' Seminar in the spring. Each student's respective preceptor acts as his advisor on this project.

C. By memory:
   (a) St. Matthew 5:3-12, "The Beatitudes"
   (b) St. John 1:1-5, "The Word"
   (c) I Corinthians 13, "The Greatest of These"
   (d) Shakespeare, "The quality of mercy is not strained"
      from *The Merchant of Venice*
   (e) Shakespeare, "To be, or not to be: that is the question"
      from *Hamlet*

GRADE 11:
  I. MATHS AND SCIENCES
     A. Pre-calculus: trigonometry, analytic geometry, and pre-calculus (1/9)
     B. Project Physics (2/9)*
  II. ARTS AND LANGUAGES
     A. Fine Arts: see Grade 7 (1/9)†
     B. Performing Arts: see Grade 7 (1/9)†
     C. Greek III, Russian III, Latin V, French V, etc. (1/9)
  III. HUMANE LETTERS (3/9)
     A. Outline texts: Harrison/Sullivan, *A Short History of Western Civilization*
        Palmer and Colton, *History of the Modern World*
        Weber, *The Western Tradition*
        Durant, *The Lessons of History*
        H. Coombes, *Literature and Criticism*

        Bacon, from *Essays*: "Of Truth," "Of Marriage and Single Life,"
          "Of Studies"
        from *Novum Organum*: "The Idols" #50-68
        Galileo, Letter to Madame Christina of Lorraine: "Concerning the Use
          of Biblical Quotations in matters of Science"
          The Trial of Galileo (selections)

        Milton, *Paradise Lost* (selections)
          Samson Agonistes (with historical notes)
          "Areopagitica"
        Gibbon, *Autobiography*
        Voltaire, *Candide*
        Kant, "What Is Enlightenment?"
        Rousseau, *Confessions* (abridged)

        Rousseau, "The Social Contract"
        Hume, "Of the Original Contract"
        Locke, "True End of Civil Government"
        Hobbes, *Leviathan* (selections)
        Swift, *Gulliver's Travels* (selections)
        Wordsworth, *The Prelude*, books IX, X, XI (on France)

        Tolstoy, *War and Peace*
        Stendhal, *The Red and the Black*
        Goethe, *Faust*, pt. 1
        A. J. P. Taylor, *Bismarck*

---

*Lab sciences occupy six periods a week, four classes and two laboratories.
†Meets in two-period blocks twice a week.

Gogol, *Dead Souls*
Lermontov, *A Hero of our Time*
Dostoyevsky, *Crime and Punishment*

Coleridge, "Rhyme of the Ancient Mariner"
Brontë, *Wuthering Heights*
Hardy, *The Return of the Native*
Conrad, *Heart of Darkness*

Dickens, *Hard Times*
Dostoyevsky, "The Grand Inquisitor"
Wilde, *The Importance of Being Earnest*
Tuchman, *The Proud Tower*
Marx and Engels, "The Communist Manifesto"
Ibsen, *An Enemy of the People*
Chekhov, *The Cherry Orchard*
Shaw, *Man and Superman*

Trotsky, *The Russian Revolution* (sel. and ed. by F. W. Dupee)

Zamiatin, *We*

Siegfried Sassoon, *Selected Poems*
Wilfred Owen, *Selected Poems*
Remarque, *All Quiet on the Western Front*
Graves, *Good-bye to All That*

Yeats, *Selected Poems*
Strachey, *Eminent Victorians*
Joyce, *Portrait of the Artist as a Young Man*
Freud, *The Origin and Development of Psychoanalysis*

Kafka, "The Penal Colony"
Camus, *The Stranger*
E. H. Carr, *The Twenty Years' Crisis, 1919-1939*
Bullock, *Hitler: A Study in Tyranny*

Fowles, *The Magus*

B. Research paper topic: each student is expected to write a short thesis of 3,000 to 5,000 words in one of the following (International Baccalaureate) areas:

    (a) The causes, practices, and effects of wars
    (b) The economic problems of the interwar period
    (c) The rise and rule of single-party dictatorships

(d) Decolonization and the rise of new nations

(e) The development of the technological culture

This thesis is submitted to the Grade 11 Teachers' Seminar in the spring. Grade 11 teachers act as thesis advisors.

C. By memory:

(a) Marvell, "To His Coy Mistress"

(b) Blake, "A Poison Tree"

(c) Keats, "Ode to a Nightingale"

(d) Tennyson, "Strong Son of God, Immortal Love" from *In Memoriam A.H.H.*

(e) Hopkins, "The Habit of Perfection"

(f) Hardy, "In Time of the Breaking of Nations"

(g) Arnold, "Dover Beach"

(h) Yeats, "The Second Coming"

(i) Spender, "I Think Continually of Those Who Were Truly Great"

GRADE 12:

I. MATHS AND SCIENCES*

A. Calculus	(1/9) Preferred
B. Biology II	(2/9) Preferred
C. Chemistry II	(2/9)
D. Physics II	(2/9)
E. Probability and Statistics	(1/9)
F. Astronomy	(1/9)
G. Introduction to Economics	(1/9)
H. History of Maths and Sciences	(1/9)

II. ARTS AND LANGUAGES*

A. Fine Arts: see Grade 7 (1/9)†

B. Performing Arts: see Grade 7 (1/9)†

C. Greek IV, Russian IV, Latin VI, French VI, etc. (1/9)

D. Independent Study: with permission. (1/9)

III. PROBLEMS OF KNOWLEDGE AND OF FAITH (1/9)

Plato, *Phaedo*

Republic

Symposium

Aristotle, *Ethics*

---

*All Grade 12 Maths and Sciences are electives. Foreign language and independent study are electives in the Arts and Languages. Seniors must fill five-ninths of their schedule from Maths and Sciences and Arts and Languages, making it possible for a senior to study three-ninths Maths and Sciences and two-ninths Arts and Languages, or vice versa.

†Meets in two-period blocks twice a week.

Paul, Epistle to the Romans
First Epistle to the Corinthians
Clement of Rome, "First Epistle to the Corinthians"
Selections from Origen, Basil of Caesarea, and Gregory of Nyssa
Augustine, *City of God*, Book 8
Chesterton, *The Everlasting Man*
Schumacher, *A Guide for the Perplexed*

IV. HUMANE LETTERS (3/9)
A. Outline texts: Bailyn et al., *The Great Republic*
Morison, *Oxford History of the American People*
Hofstadter, *Great Issues in American History*

Franklin, *The Autobiography* (selections)
Hamilton, *The Federalist*
The Constitution

de Tocqueville, *Democracy in America*
Emerson, "The American Scholar"
"Self-Reliance"
Thoreau, *Walden*
Melville, *Moby Dick*
Whitman, "Song of Myself"
Twain, *Huckleberry Finn*
W. Jordon, *White Over Black* (abridged)

Freeman, *Lee's Lieutenants* (selections)
Whitman, *Specimen Days*
Markham, "Lincoln, the Man of the People"

B. Hart, "The Luck of Roaring Camp"
"The Outcasts of Poker Flat"
S. Crane, "The Bride Comes to Yellow Sky"
Turner, "The Significance of the Frontier in American History"

Dickenson, *Selected Poems*
H. James, *The American*
H. Adams, *The Education of Henry Adams*
Frost, *Selected Poems*

Eliot, "The Love-Song of J. Alfred Prufrock"
"The Wasteland"
Pound, "The White Stag"
"The Return"
"Portrait d'une femme"
"Mauberley"

H. Crane, "Black Tambourine"
    "Repose of Rivers"
    "The Bridge"
Agee, *Let Us Now Praise Famous Men*

O'Neill, *Long Day's Journey into Night*
Anderson, *Winesburg, Ohio*
Cather, "Neighbor Rosicky"
O'Connor, "The Life You Save May Be Your Own"
    "A Good Man Is Hard To Find"
Faulkner, *The Unvanquished*
Miller, *Death of a Salesman*

Warren, *All the King's Men*
Ellison, *Invisible Man*

Ortega y Gasset, *The Revolt of the Masses*
Kafka, *Amerika*
Niebuhr, *The Irony of American History*
Halberstam, *The Best and the Brightest*
Skinner, *Walden Two*
B. Spring film series: "Citizen Kane"
    "Dodsworth"
    "All the King's Men"
    "Streetcar Named Desire"
    "The Grapes of Wrath"
    "The Caine Mutiny"
    "Casablanca"
    "The Quiet American"
Readings from: Max Lerner, *America as a Civilization*
C. By memory:
    (a) Lincoln, "Gettysburg Address"
    (b) Whitman, "I celebrate myself"
    (c) MacLeish, "You, Andrew Marvell"
    (d) Frost, "Stopping By Woods"
    (e) Crane, "Repose of Rivers"
    (f) Stevens, "The Emperor of Ice Cream"
    (g) Auden, "Musée des Beaux Arts"
    (h) Warren, "Bearded Oaks"
    (i) Markham, "The Man with a Hoe"

Weekly Class Schedule

	Mon.	Tue.	Wed.	Thur.	Fri.
8:00-8:50	1	8	6	4	2
8:55-9:45	2	9	7	5	3
9:50-10:40	3	1	8	9	8
10:45-11:05	Activities-Assembly Period				
11:10-12:00	4	2	9	6	4
12:05-12:55	5	3	1	7	5
1:00-1:20	First Lunch Period				
1:20-1:40	Second Lunch Period				
1:45-2:35	6	4	2	8	6
2:40-3:30	7	5	3	1	7
3:45-5:00	Athletic Program				

Notes: Period 9, which meets only three times a week, is always a Humane Letters class. This offers assembly and lecture possibilities either by class, by grade, or by school, particularly on Wednesday and Thursday, when Period 9 abuts the regularly scheduled Assembly Period. Period 9 also affords time for interclass debates and for visiting teachers from Maths and Sciences or Arts and Languages.

Periods 2-3, 4-5, and 6-7 always follow in uninterrupted sequence, making them natural slots for lab sciences and arts. Fine Arts and Performing Arts generally share one of these sequences, so that a student may have Fine Arts during 4-5 on Monday and Thursday, and have Performing Arts during 4-5 on Tuesday and Friday.

There must be one period that is free for all preceptors in a given grade when the Teachers' Seminar can meet.

10

SOME QUESTIONS AND ASSUMPTIONS (WHAT OUGHT TO BE)

For there is no doubt that the most radical division that it is possible to make of humanity is that which splits it into two classes of creatures: those who make great demands on themselves, piling up difficulties and duties; and those who demand nothing special of themselves, but for whom to live is to be every moment what they already are, without imposing on themselves any effort towards perfection; mere buoys that float on the waves. . . . The decisive matter is whether we attach our life to one or the other vehicle, to a maximum or a minimum of demands upon ourselves.

—José Ortega y Gasset

I

Behind every educational program lie certain questions and assumptions. The quality of these and the imaginative deliberation with which they are put into practice determine the quality of the school. If they are not regularly articulated and evaluated, they lose their efficacy, and the school loses its integrating vision, normative power, and dialectical vitality. The whole purpose of education becomes obscured, and the school begins to respond with perilous inconsistency to the selfish and conflicting demands of its constituent parts. It is critical, therefore, that we bare our questions and assumptions before going on to explain and defend the preceding proposal.

To begin with, there is no such thing as a universal or objective set of questions about the school. Questions originate in an individual's thought, no matter how uncontroversial or concrete the experience bringing them to mind — and they play a creative role in shaping their own answers. The best questions, it seems to me, are those least prejudiced by the availability of pat answers, as well

122

as those originating not only in practice but in imaginative theory. In other words, the best questions are not limited by what can be done; they ask what ought to be done, knowing that the former question — although scientifically correct — can only make a poor education worse by narrowing the range of inquiry and by limiting the possibilities for improvement. Also, since our practical faults often originate in our questions, we must articulate these questions and thereby risk exposing our pedagogical biases so that we and those we serve can recognize our faults and trace error to its source for a proper prognosis.

So, with these conditions in mind and remembering the idea with which we began (that there are questions possessing a wisdom apart from answers), here are some of the questions I think it worth putting to school administrators and teachers:

(I)   To administrators:

1.   Priorities: What are your school's priorities? How does your school determine and assign its priorities? How clearly and effectively are these communicated to the faculty, to parents, to students, and — where applicable — to candidates for admission?

2.   Organization: Is your school organized to reflect its priorities? For example, if you believe that ongoing scholarship is important to good teaching, does your school's curriculum and budget reflect this commitment? If you believe that your students ought to be able to write with style and precision, does your school's organization testify to this belief? Are your students always writing, and is your faculty at leisure to give their writing careful and personal criticism?

3.   Community: How do you challenge your faculty to maintain spiritual and intellectual growth, to burn always with a gemlike flame, to infect their students and colleagues with a curiosity in ideas and an enthusiasm for the life of the mind? What steps must be taken to give your school a friendly, serious, and purposeful environment: a context in which the influence of ideas and of mature personalities can be felt *outside* the classroom, as well as inside?

4.   Purposes: How do you keep before your faculty the purposes of a whole education, which are so often hidden in a forest of methodology and of administrative apparatus? To what extent is your faculty engaged in a dialogue enhancing its self-awareness and its understanding of the critical relation between the normative and the analytical phases of learning?

(II)   To teachers:

1. Writing: How do you teach better writing and more intelligent communication?

2. Thinking: How do you teach clear, forthright, incisive thinking? How do you go beyond the mere stroking of sensibility to the enlivening of intelligence? How do you give your students a more critical attitude toward what they read, see, or hear?

3. Knowing: Are your students taught to distinguish among the various species of knowledge and to appreciate the uses and limitations of each? Are your students alive to their needs for poetic truth, as well as scientific truth, religious truth, and historical truth?

4. Questions: How do you teach the important questions? How do you provoke from your students the important questions? How do you know the important questions? How does the scholarly community ensure that you are asking the questions that a rigorous commitment to normative learning demands?

5. Communication: How and on what level does your faculty communicate with one another? How well do you know what your students are studying outside your class or what they have read and what questions they have developed before entering your class for the first time?

6. Attitudes: What is your opinion of yourself as a teacher? What do you believe to be your true competence? Do you have an all-knowing manner in the classroom, or are your methods dialectical? How much reading and reflection precedes your entrance into the classroom? How much do you learn in the classroom? How often do you ask your students questions to which you do not presume to have ready answers? How eager are you to learn from your colleagues or to examine ideas outside your chosen discipline? How often do you encourage students to look beyond the borders of your particular academic discipline?

7. Students: How well do you know your students? If you do not know them well, what might that say about your attitude toward them and toward teaching? How might that attitude affect your ability to teach effectively?

8. Responsibility: Why are your best students often the most arrogant and the least sensitive to the lively connection between ideas and action, between knowledge and responsibility, and between ability and humility? What can you do to make this connection more compelling? Do you take responsibility outside the classroom for developing the conscience and style of your students?

9. Time: Can and do you make time to get to know your students and their parents, to engage in scholarship under and outside the rubric of the curriculum or of the academic discipline, and to discuss fertile ideas with your colleagues and students? Do your students have time to get to know you, to reflect on their studies, to read beyond the syllabus, and to pursue ideas in informal conversations with you? If so, are they encouraged to use their time thus?

10. Self-evaluation: What makes one educational experience better than another? Do you keep a written record of your teaching methods' successes and failures? Do you share this wisdom with your colleagues? How?

11. Values: When we fail to make the connection between our disciplinary parts and the whole of knowledge, education becomes valueless: bled of meaning for the individual. The hand cannot be studied apart from the body. The accumulation of discrete parts of knowledge does not add up to wisdom, that is, a workable understanding of where each part fits into the structured pattern of the whole. This dialectical principle suggests more questions: Do you understand your disciplinary parts and are you teaching them in relation to the whole of knowledge? Are you teaching what you *can* or what you *should*, the way you *can* or the way you *should*? Are you avoiding questions that lead you into other academic disciplines? Are you consciously predicating analysis upon a normative inquiry?

(III)   To administrators and teachers:

1.   Parents: What is the role of parents and of the home in your program of study?

2.   Change: How does your school respond to change? How does it evaluate change? How does it articulate its problems and to whom? Are the lines of accountability clearly drawn? Is the school organized in such a way as to account for growth in its methods and experiments, or does change imply a static transfer of power and ideas within the school?

3.   Subject matter: Is there a more rational sequence for the introduction of subject matter into the curriculum? On what basis is subject matter chosen: for student interest or ability, for faculty interest or expertise, for developing certain skills in the student, or in the interests of *paideia*? How often do you consider the nature of what you teach on a schoolwide basis?

4.   Scholarship: What is the connection between ongoing scholarship and good teaching? What might be the benefits of a purposeful sabbatical program in the secondary school?

5. Leadership: Is your school a "leader" school? Why? What is it doing that other schools are not — given the peculiar capabilities of its students and faculty?

6. Ideals: What is your school's ideal image of itself, of its teachers, and of its students? Is your school organized to stimulate the achievement of these ideals?

7. Paideia: How do you define the person that you wish your graduate to be? What are his or her peculiar virtues? What is valuable and enduring about your school's stamp upon the student? What have you given your students to live for, or die with?

II

Before listing the assumptions upon which my proposal is founded, it is fitting to point out that an original assumption is perhaps the rarest thing in the world. All men live on borrowed assumptions, but no man boasts of it. For this reason, to imply that schools can be built upon sets of critical questions is somewhat misleading, for even the questions we ask spring from our assumptions about life and learning. What distinguishes one man's thinking and activity from another's is not the originality of his assumptions or his lack of them, but his conscious choice and arrangement of assumptions, as well as, sometimes, his knowledge of their sources. By the same token, however, it is difficult to imagine the hatching of an assumption without a question calling it into being.

The modern era suffers in two extremes over the nature of assumptions. The first extreme is born of an attitude contemptuous of the past and its unscientific ways. It expects to unearth an original set of assumptions upon which to construct the modern school. This extreme may be said to represent the sanguine position of the educational romantics and progressives. The second extreme shares the progressive's contempt for the past, but it despairs of discovering a new set of assumptions or of having any control over assumptions and their alleged effects whatsoever. The assumption is merely a reflex conditioned by the special characteristics of one's corner of the material universe. To some extent, the assumption can be controlled by reshaping one's corner, but this pedagogical back door begs the question — Who does the shaping, and what are his assumptions? — while presuming the shaper's ability to transcend his own reflexive conditioning. This may be said to represent the grim position of the educational behaviorists.

I mention, with no intention of fighting, this contemporary duel to mark off the unfashionable middle ground upon which I stand. My assumptions cannot boast originality because they are rooted in man's hard-won and meticulously preserved knowledge of his unchanging human nature. The belief in something called "human nature" is itself an assumption that both progressives and behaviorists deplore; yet no education can hope to transform — or even develop — man's manifold potentials without first understanding him in all his natural domains — the individual, the social, and the religious.

Nor is there any reason to admit the inevitability or inefficacy of man's assumptions, as the behaviorist would insist. There is something both unique and potentially world transforming about every thoughtful person's choice and ordering of assumptions. To deny this paradox flies in the face of history. The only validity of the behaviorist hypothesis is as a self-fulfilling prophecy, for surely those who cease to believe in their freedom to order assumptions creatively and to act upon them imaginatively will fail to accomplish anything for having tried nothing. In fact, as Kant argued, this fanciful hypothesis, although tantalizingly demonstrable in reason and in experiment with certain subhuman species, is in human practice impossible. One cannot even entertain the hypothesis without assuming his freedom to do so. Yet the Cartesian determination to unlock the mystery of human existence by fastening on some isolated aspect of thought or experience — whether on man's satirical predictability or his romantic spontaneity — is ever with us.

Finally, my choice and ordering of assumptions may be dismissed as "idealistic" because they fail to meet the inviolable "givens" of the contemporary educational scene. To be idealistic is to commit the unpardonable sin of asking what ought to be done in seeming indifference to the limitations on what can be done. This cuts across the grain of the modern world by forcing analysis to serve the normative inquiry. But the true educator, I believe, is never satisfied with the givens. Rather than ask, "What are the givens?," he demands, "Why are these the givens, and how can they be changed to make our imperative course of action possible?" The so-called givens, whether of human nature or of institutional feasibility, are precisely what the true educator wishes to transform — while in the theorizing of the modern social scientist, they become the ally rather than the adversary of reform.

The sometimes idealistic assumptions, then, that undergird my proposal for the modern practice of classical education are the following:

1.   The need to prepare students for future employment is overtaken by a liberal education. Cardinal Newman's (1969) description of liberal education remains, to this day, unimpeachable: that which teaches the student "to see things as they are, to go right to the point, to disentangle a skein of thought, to detect what is sophistical, and to discard what is irrelevant. It prepares him to fill any post with credit, and to master any subject with facility."

2.   Before he is 18, no one has time to do more than a few things well; therefore, better to teach a few subjects thoroughly than to force a child to be a mediocrity in many subjects, destroying his standards, obscuring the nature of mastery, and concealing the measure of his ignorance. The school is not preeminently a place where the child is exposed to a kaleidoscope of new ideas,

but where he is given the direction, the discipline, and the methods to master basic ideas and where art, science, and letters are studied with the intention of forming the student's conscience and style.

3. "To be in command of these basic ideas," writes Jerome Bruner (1966) of Harvard, "to use them effectively, requires a continual deepening of one's understanding of them that comes from learning to use them in progressively more complex forms." Basic skills and ideals should be introduced very early in a child's education and enlarged in subsequent years by reintroducing them at higher levels of complexity and abstraction.

4. Any subject, no matter how potentially complex, can be taught to any student at any level. The secret is not in what is taught, but in how it is taught. The compromise to the student's level of psychological development should be made by altering the teaching method rather than by substituting facile subject matter.

5. "Effective education," Richard Weaver (1964) maintains, "often demands the rigorous suppressing of a present, desultory interest so that we can focus on things that have real, enduring, and sanctioned interest." The curriculum of the effective school does not duck the issue of selectivity, but addresses it comprehensively and coherently. It is the folly of many modern schools to neglect to provide the focus necessary for disciplining its students' minds and wills. By forfeiting their duty to shape the curriculum and by leaving selectivity up to departments within the school or to individuals within departments, these schools insure an inconsistent, hit-or-miss approach to education that is bound to frustrate the conscientious student, aggravate the idealistic teacher, and make *paideia* impossible.

6. The selection of subject matter must be governed by Vergerius' principle: "Begin with the best" (Origo 1960). Students learn excellence through the excellence of their models. "Nothing — not all the knowledge in the world —" writes Sir Richard Livingston (1950), "educates like the vision of greatness, and nothing can take its place."

7. Responsible learning requires a profound and intimate teacher-pupil relationship wherein the normative connection between knowledge and responsibility can be made. A personality that embodies and evokes *paideia* is a window on the world of arts and letters and sciences. "The general principles of any study you may learn by books at home; but the detail, the colour, the tone, the air, the life which makes it live for us, you must catch all these from those in whom it lives already" (Livingston 1950).

8. The tendentious debate between freedom and discipline in education can only thrive in the absence of an intimate relationship between the pupil and

the teacher. The compassion and love of the teacher for the pupil and the respect and affection of the pupil for the teacher resolve this debate by transcending it in the dialectic of classical education.

9. Only the careless and unskilled teacher answers questions before they are asked. The teacher's chief task is to provoke the question, not to answer it; to cultivate in his students an active curiosity, not to inundate them in factual information. The teacher's answers will not stimulate the formation of conscience and style in his student, nor will they impart *paideia*, if they are not in response to the student's own questions.

10. The teacher's true competence is not in his mastery of a subject, but in his ability to provoke the right questions and get into a new subject quickly and incisively. Although this competence derives from the teacher's understanding of the nature of mastery — having mastered at least one subject himself — it implies the teacher's peculiar eagerness to explore new subjects and new ideas with his students. What students can most hope to learn from a good teacher is how to approach a new subject with the aim of mastering it.

11. The normative approach to learning draws the analytical after it, whereas the analytical approach repels the normative. The fragmentation of arts and letters into academic disciplines (literature, history, philosophy, religion, social studies, and so forth) answers an analytical need that pushes normative inquiry into the interstices between disciplines. This is the strongest argument for reuniting the arts and letters.

12. The failure of numerous interdisciplinary endeavors results from the doctrinaire effort to treat arts and letters analytically — an effort symbolized by the team-teaching concept, wherein each member of the team presumes to have only a partial knowledge of the whole subject being taught. So long as this analytical bias persists, the reunification of arts and letters is foredoomed.

13. The structure of a curriculum must correspond to a process of development in the body of knowledge. "Development is a *continuous* process," John Dewey (Archambault 1964) writes, "and continuity signifies consecutiveness of action. Here was the strong point of traditional education at its best. The subject matter of the classics and mathematics involved of necessity, for those who mastered it, a consecutive and orderly development along definite lines."

14. Much learning is misspent because it is not placed within a thoughtfully structured pattern. This pattern not only assists memory, which is the result of having learned something properly, but it helps to motivate the student by unfolding to him the purposes of his education. (The runner runs best on a clearly marked course.) Thus does Jerome Bruner (1966) observe that "the more

one has a sense of structure of a subject, the more densely packed and longer a learning episode one can get through without fatigue." This observation can be enlarged to include the entire curriculum.

15. The craze for guidance counseling in the modern school is in large measure an unwitting acknowledgement that education is failing to make the strategic connection between what a student learns in the classroom and what choices he makes outside the classroom. The modern mode of instruction undercuts responsible learning because of its analytical attack on subject matter and because of its utilitarian self-justification. Learning has lost its normative edge, and we need special guidance to make our students responsible, self-aware persons. But guidance counseling cannot begin to perform the *morphosis* of a healthy *paideia* — for students acquire a lively sense of values implicitly, not extrinsically, when normative inquiry is a part of every class and discipline, not the special study of one.

16. "Religious truth is not only a portion but a condition of general knowledge," wrote Newman (Gaebelein 1976). The history of God's revelation in Christ and the progress of Christianity are too central to the development of Western *paideia* to be isolated from the study of arts and letters. Such a separation emasculates the study of religion, as well as of the arts and letters.

17. The school should not nurture and ape the attitudes and beliefs of popular culture — what Erasmus (1965) calls "the false opinions and vicious predilections of the masses" — but it must call these into question with the inherited wisdom of its lofty *paideia*, its vision of greatness, its ideals of conscience and style. The school best serves society when it establishes itself as the secondary aspect of contradiction in a dialectical relationship with the state and popular culture.

18. The school's organization bespeaks the level of its dialectical commitment. Where there is no structure for an active dialectic within the school, there can be no external dialectic with society or with the state. This means that everyone involved in a classical education is a student, whether teacher or pupil, for only the example of a teacher's learning evokes the creative tension necessary for an effective dialectic within the school.

19. Education as *paideia* is not preparation for life, for college, or for work; it is our inherited means of living fully in the present, while we grow in wisdom and in grace, in conscience and in style, entering gradually into "the good life."

11

THREE SCHOOLS IN ONE ACADEMY

*In any whole consisting of parts a loss of harmony between
the parts is paid for by the whole in a corresponding loss
of self-determination.*

—Arnold Toynbee

I

It is reasonable as well as convenient to divide the classical academy into three
schools under one roof: the school of maths and sciences, the school of arts
and languages, and the school of humane letters. Harmony among these three
schools and within each school is essential; therefore, the classical curriculum
reflects the shared purposes of all three schools. All schools serve the normative
goals of the whole academy: to form the conscience and style of each student
through the study of great art, basic science, and good letters. The curriculum
encourages the academy to meet these goals, while discouraging one school or
academic discipline from strengthening itself at the expense of another. Within
the framework of a unified and comprehensive curriculum, each school can
afford to be creative *in its teaching methods* without endangering the balance
and self-determination of the whole academy.

By contrast, from the eclectic curriculum of the modern school flows an
ocean one inch deep. There seems no end to the diversity of the modern school's
course offerings and no limit to the educator's eagerness to obliterate curricular
shores and to accommodate the desires of teachers, students, parents, experts,
and state bureaucrats. With no regulating body of knowledge to impose a
pattern, curriculum development becomes a euphemism for vague consensus,
eclecticism, elaborate self-study, theorization, and a belief that experience need
not be qualified to be educative. The barren shores of learning jut in and out
without unity or design. Were it not for the benison of limited resources, one

131

imagines that there would be no reason at all to resist the demands for expanding the curriculum or to set up some criteria for selectivity.

Yet the wider the ocean of course offerings, the narrower the education of the individual student. When left to himself, the student, who by definition lacks knowledge and mature discernment, often impoverishes his own learning by selecting studies that already interest or come easily to him rather than those that expand his interest and challenge him. The school that widens its curriculum polishes its own image at the high risk of tarnishing the individual student's actual program of study. Not only is this appearance of academic riches deceiving and detrimental to the real education of the student, it dissipates the limited resources and energies of the school. One can be sure that the school must pay for its elegant dessert dishes in the form of cheaper cuts of meat. A species of Gresham's Law comes into play, with bad courses driving out good.

It is not a privilege but the obligation of the school's administration and faculty to establish a curriculum for accomplishing their normative purposes. In fulfilling this obligation, the framers of the curriculum ought to remember that a curriculum does not serve the school; it serves the individual student. Its purpose is not good publicity for the institution, but *paideia* for the young person whom they educate, with the expectation that he will someday educate them. They must know that a democratic curriculum does not educate responsible, self-governing citizens for democracy and that the adolescent mind should not be permitted to delimit the knowledge and abilities of the grown man. There can be no *morphosis* without a mold and no *paideia* without a unified and coherent curriculum.

In framing my proposal for a unified curriculum, I have asked myself: How does a scholar's mind work? Why is it that the excitement of scholarship usually comes so late, if ever, in the modern student's life? A scholarly mind is characterized by an ability to make connections, to visualize the relatedness of sundry facts, ideas, and concepts. The scholar's mind works like a person laboring over a jigsaw puzzle, grouping pieces by pattern, image, and color, while retaining in the mind an outline of the whole picture. The scholar derives his excitement and motivation at first from snapping discrete pieces together and, in time, from seeing the image of the whole puzzle begin to emerge. His excitement, as well as his chances for completing the puzzle, however, depend on his being given a sufficient number of pieces from the same puzzle.

The joy of learning arrives too late in the modern student's life because the eclectic curriculum tosses out random pieces of knowledge from any number of different puzzles. There is no structured pattern for the initial ordering of pieces, and the student is years, if ever, in sorting out the pieces and their respective puzzles. The natural motivation for scholarship — the excitement of making connections and of seeing the whole emerge from a relation of parts — is lost; and the school must turn to an elaborate and ineffectual system of punishments and rewards to motivate its students.

Many writers have commented upon the prolonged adolescence and dependency of American youth and the sense of frustration and worthlessness accompanying this phenomenon. The eclectic curriculum of the modern school promotes this pathetic state of affairs by aggravating the young person's sense of helplessness and confusion in the face of a growing mass of information and opinion. Because of his cluttered, disorderly mind — helpless to make the fundamental connections between basic ideas or to find reference points for its inchoate sensibilities — the young person cannot participate intelligently in the public debate over the great issues confronting his nation and his times. So the young person joins a swelling number of Americans whose eclectic, superficial education bars them from participating independently and imaginatively in the decisions transforming their lives and liberties.

The beauty of the classical curriculum is that it dwells on one problem, one author, or one epoch long enough to allow even the youngest student a chance to exercise his mind in a scholarly way: to make connections and to trace developments, lines of reasoning, patterns of action, recurring symbolisms, plots, and motifs. At Vittorino da Feltre's school in Mantua, for instance, the education of the youngest scholars was based on only four authors: Virgil, Homer, Cicero, and Demosthenes. Not until they had mastered these were his pupils allowed to pass on to Ovid, Lucan, Xenophon, and Herodotus.

This recognition of how the scholarly mind works, perhaps more than any insight into the nature of knowledge itself, supports Johann Herbart's claim that the "stages in the curriculum should correspond to historical evolution" (McLachlan 1970). The curriculum should begin in some limited sphere, feeding the student from all sides (art, history, literature, religion, and so forth) with pieces to one puzzle (the Middle Ages, for instance). This puzzle will itself become a piece in later and larger puzzles (an understanding of the Middle Ages contributing to the student's emerging picture of the Italian Renaissance, and a knowledge of the Italian Renaissance forming part of the design of Reformation Europe, and so forth). The measured unfolding of history is an ideal vehicle for providing this insight into the connectedness of knowledge's parts and for encouraging the student to perform creative acts of scholarship at an early age. History embraces the whole of knowledge, as well as the student himself, but its vastness need not frighten or overawe the novice. At the beginning, it can be treated, as it was by the ancients, as mythology: the same questions can be asked of Churchill as of Tolkien. Being full of discrete puzzles comprising pieces to ever larger puzzles, history affords an almost immediate opportunity for the student to exercise his or her incipient ability to make connections.

Because the student himself is a part of it, the study of history lends itself to normative inquiry, bridging in exciting and ennobling stories the hiatus between knowledge and responsibility. No subject matter deserving of praise as excellent in form or in content is excluded from the study of history, and no curriculum framed in history should fail to form a quick, intuitive, scholarly mind: a mind trained in discourse and thought, not solitary research, and able to participate in public debates over the great issues facing the nation and the times. Students will know the meaning of excellence by having been schooled in the excellencies of the past, and they will join the great debates of their (and all) times on the strength of a mind educated to grasp the connectedness of things and to understand the fragments of modern life that take their meaning and value from one's dialectical comprehension of the whole. It is, therefore, neither in the quality of the subject matter nor in the sequence of its presentation that concessions should first be made to the unformed adolescent mind. Rather, the impersonal, analytical methods of the modern school must accede to the personal, normative methods of classical education if our young are going to read the classics of their civilization with enjoyment, understanding, and benefit.

II

The heart of the classical academy, then, is the school of humane letters. In it, the study of literature, grammar, history, philosophy, religion, and the social sciences occurs in one class and under one teacher. This arrangement allows a drastic reduction in the total number of students assigned to each teacher. Under the present system, for instance, if three teachers have 90 students apiece in, say, the separate classes of history, literature, and religion, in the school of humane letters these teachers will have only 30 students apiece. This reorganization also raises the number of contact-hours between the student and his teacher from, say, four hours per week under the present system to 11 hours per week in the school of humane letters – and all of this can be accomplished with the same overall student-faculty ratio.

The humane letters teacher, instead of having three or four different classes, prepares for only one class of 30 students, which he meets in groups of ten, eight times a week, and in a class of 30, three times a week (during Period 9). The student inhabits four concentric circles within the school of humane letters: the school itself, the grade within the school, the 30-member class within the grade, and the ten-member group within the class. Most of the student's work is done in the ten-member group, but three times a week, he joins his teacher's other two groups during Period 9 for intergroup debates or for a class or a lecture. On occasion, the school gathers during Period 9 either by grade or by school to attend a lecture, concert, play, or other presentation pertinent to the study of the humane letters. In the school of humane letters, then, the teacher spends more time with fewer students, as well as less time preparing for different classes and grading innumerable student exercises. At least twice a day, the student returns to the school of humane letters to a teacher whom he knows well and who acts as his advisor and "moral tutor" and to a subject that focuses and structures the rest of his work in the classical academy.

The benefits of this reorganization are manifold. First, the unity of academic disciplines enables a young student to exercise his mind in a scholarly way. The excitement of making connections motivates the student, as well as the teacher, who no longer dispenses predigested chunks of information from a daily lesson plan or from a specialized knowledge gleaned years ago. Teaching many subjects as one challenges the teacher to continue to learn, while honing his true competence as a teacher: his ability to provoke the right questions from his students and to show them how to approach a new subject with the aim of mastering it. His act of teaching in the school of humane letters shows a living scholarship.

Second, a greatly reduced total number of students per teacher allows the humane letters teacher to make regular writing assignments, while availing him of the time to grade his students' writing carefully, to return it with personal commentary, and to monitor closely the progress of the individual student. The comprehensive humane letters teacher focuses the work of the student, who is no longer shuttled from class to class, teacher to teacher, and assignment to assignment in a frenzy of noisy activity. Because the student is now responsible to one teacher instead of three for his work in the humane letters, his efforts for the teacher are intensified, balanced, and individually directed.

The organization of the school of humane letters also fosters the ideal of a profound and intimate relationship between teacher and student wherein the student's efforts are comprehensively directed and personally rewarded. The school whose fragmented curriculum condemns this relationship loses the idiosyncratic, intimate, and moral character of a normative environment; it must direct by anarchy or tyranny and reward with quantitative gradations of success or failure. Teacher and student must exist in a superficial "means" relationship, as they often do in the modern school: the one as a means for the teacher's livelihood; the other, a means for the student's advancement. Both are judged by the cold quantification of academic performance. The busy teacher neglects his gifted students, believing that with these he has succeeded or at least cannot fail, and he occupies the few spare moments with the weak or unmotivated students. On the basis of a merely academic performance, the gifted student basks in the illusion of himself as a superior being, and the inferior student eventually rejects the pursuit of knowledge as a pastime without meaning to the person who cannot perform at an acceptable level. For both, learning is just a hurdle (or barrier) to later status and wealth.

The modern teacher, trapped in this environment where only the "professional" relationship with a student is either applauded or possible, cannot communicate learning's transcendent, normative worth. He cannot judge or even afford to care whether his students are made better, fuller, or richer persons by their learning; instead, the multiple-choice test must tell the whole story. But that the true test of an idea is in deeds is an expression of the relationship between a teacher and his students, not of the idea in academic isolation. Only within the context of a profound and intimate teacher-student relationship can the school accomplish its normative purposes, joining the classroom to life and knowledge to responsibility.

Lastly, the organization of the school of humane letters assures the normative emphasis of an effective *paideia*. While disciplinary unification and classical literature make it easier to raise questions of value, only a close relationship between teacher and student renders these questions themselves valuable and allows the teacher to introduce a meaningful analysis into the normative quest for understanding. Normative inquiry, to achieve its full effect, must pass between persons with confidence and respect in each other. Both the person who questions and the person who answers must act in good faith, with deep concern for the influence of their deeds and ideas on the other. This good faith and deep concern sustain the dialectic of *paideia* and develop a sense of conscience and style in both teacher and student. Like the ancient *eros*, good faith and deep concern describe a moral climate in which one finds responsible learning. In this climate, students inhale knowledge and sound judgment in the very air they breathe.

III

What of the school of humane letter's syllabus? Why should young people be made to read old books? The modern prejudice against the so-called classics is easier to explain than to justify. On the one hand, there are many who have never read the old books and who assume them to be irrelevant in content and inaccessible in form. On the other hand, there are a few who have splashed about in them or who have waded into them with erudite commentaries and works of criticism and who feel that the abstruse meanings of these dusty tomes must inevitably escape the appreciation of the young reader. Theirs is a variation on the proverbial "pearls-before-swine" argument. Behind this argument lurks the misconception that a classic is admired for its profundity — that it cannot please or benefit the reader who cannot fathom its murky depths. Modern scholarship promotes this misconception by scorning to read the classics on a normative or even descriptive level. Yet the monsters in *Beowulf*, to my knowledge, perplex only the graduate student who ponders their metaphysical significance. What 12-year-old worries about the appearance of monsters in a story of Viking conquests and of the struggle between good and evil? A classic like *Beowulf* endures because it tells a story more wonderfully and makes an argument more convincingly than any imitator can. Its unaffected simplicity, inimitable beauty, and incisive clarity are precisely what ought to place it at the heart of the curriculum. When fastidious doubts and analytical dredging are not allowed to muddy the waters, the surface of a classic, dancing with light, mirrors the depths of its own accord and reveals its truth at the young reader's own level of maturity and insight.

There is altogether too much pretense in the current attitude toward old books. Held in esteem for the wrong reasons by those who have not read them and by those who have read them with the wrong questions in mind (not wishing to be changed by them), the slightest allusion to classical literature interjects a somber note into any discussion of education. Eyebrows and suspicions are raised. Yet this awe-full and pretentious attitude surrounding the old books, more than their style and content, renders them inaccessible to the young reader, as well as to the intimidated teacher, who asks with false modesty: "Who am I — without a knowledge of medieval Latin or a degree in Renaissance literature — to teach the illustrious Dante?" So much modesty ignores the fact that Dante wrote *The Divine Comedy* in the language of the common man, hoping to entertain and inform a general audience, not a scholarly or specialized one. Certainly, not until teachers take delight in reading old books and show faith in their life-guiding value will students enjoy studying the classics of their civilization.

One cannot help but observe the trend in modern schools to substitute light "escape" reading for the more difficult classics. This practice is defended in the name of getting students to read. The assumption is that because students learn to read by reading, schools must provide books that students will want to read, books that will not overtax their patience, their limited vocabulary, or their even more limited intelligence. A corollary to this assumption, as we have seen, is that students cannot enjoy reading serious classics with their demanding styles and remote contents. Clearly, the classical academy rejects this thesis. Not only does it refute the notion that classics are inaccessible or unenjoyable to young readers, but it reminds us that the purpose of learning is discovery, not escape. Reading serves this purpose. It is not just a basic skill, as the advocates of the new reading trends would have us believe, but it is done for the purpose of discovery. Substituting the literature of escape for the classics is not education, but an attack on learning; it is not intellectual, but antiintellectual. It represents a capitulation to the adolescent appetites of our students and of our race.

Although over two hundred generations of humankind have put forward answers to the question — Why should young people study the classics? — there is neither an original nor universal response to it. This is perhaps as it should be, since the classics are preoccupied with timeless questions — not meaning, as is sometimes assumed, questions without answers, but questions with answers only for those who ask them in good faith and with deep concern, willing to commit their lives to working out the answers dialectically. When the times fail to take such questions seriously and attempt to embalm the classics in leather and entomb them on the shelf, occasionally appropriating the answers of a previous generation, civilization and men's lives go into decline. The present begins to spend its spiritual capital in order to sustain its (threatened) need for order and for a sense of purpose. Its literature and art reflect the drain on capital by becoming trivial and full of hollow laughter or by striving after seriousness in a dark, bitter, pessimistic tone. What is alarming about both humorous and serious art at such times is the absence of normative substance, the haunting neglect of those timeless questions buried in the old books that build spiritual capital in men and in their civilizations.

The normative concerns of the old books run against the spirit of our present age, not a terrible spirit, but a lost and pathetic one, imagining its greatest freedom to lie in the anxieties of a moral vacuum. When this poor spirit ventures to raise normative questions, believing them to be analytically unanswerable anyway, it does so without the dialectical commitment necessary for answering them. Its effete morality consists of simply having raised the question or of having discussed the "value preferences." Consequently, the pursuit of truth, as opposed to analytical fact, proceeds willy-nilly, and in the end, cynically. To raise the moral question seems as preposterous today in some settings as a firm answer to the question would have sounded a generation ago. Most educators, in fact, have given up on such questions, protesting ignorance, saying that they cannot know what ought to be but are quite confident in their ability to teach what is, thanks to the tools of science. But *what is* the human condition appears to grow darker and darker, since man is left without a map to guide his steps. Like a nightwalker who despairs of clearly discerning the objects in his path, the educator first turns his attention to his shoes and then closes his eyes.

The old books, when not burnt out in an arid analysis, will not suffer the student to close his eyes to the author's normative concerns. They do not imitate popular culture and titillate youth's prejudices and predilections, but they challenge his intelligence and sensibility, while judging his culture and his behavior against breathlessly high standards. Although it can be despoiled in an analytical shredder, the essential truth of the classic is never beyond the young person's reach. But because the classic flies above the borders of modern academic disciplines, looking down on the whole commonwealth of knowledge and not on its provincial parts, its mastery demands critical thinking rather than specialized skills. The syllabus for the school of humane letters, therefore, favors classical literature and a method of normative inquiry that tear down the analytical fences which make a patchwork of the kingdom of arts and letters.

It should be obvious that in our increasingly specialized and technological society, with family life breaking up on all sides, children need formal instruction in their humanity more than ever. The old books alone have the power to release this instruction, to shape and mold the young person in a truly human image, to give him a rich spiritual life, and to make him part of a living tradition. What is this power? Why are these ancient models so evocative? They are all informed by a tradition affirming our fundamental yearning for dignity, moral uprightness, order, freedom, purpose, and transcendent value that the modern utilitarian world does not affirm.

Moreover, the old books lay a foundation for all later learning and life. Most students go on from high school to universities, where the classics are referred to but no longer read, and all students are embarked throughout life on that great and turbulent sea of opinions belonging to themselves and to others. To examine the grounds for these opinions, whether expressed by university professors, commercial advertisers, or political demagogues, is the motive of the classics. They carry out this examination by two means. First, they expose with their piercing questions the ironies and inconsistencies attending man's false opinions and unconscious presuppositions about himself and his experiences.

In the language of the dialectic, the classic challenges analytical man's knowledge of the part with a view of the whole that puts the part in a perspective beyond the reach of analysis. At the same time, the classic presents inspiring deeds of uncompromising virtue, courage, and integrity. In this way, the old books balance the idea's doubt against the deed's dogma in a relationship that ought also to govern men's lives. Because of this marvelous dialectic at the core of old books, they best tie the knot — essential to good conduct, human happiness, and the *morphosis* of the self-governing citizen of a democracy — around knowledge and responsibility.

Before leaving this topic, a word about the particular books listed in the curriculum proposal: they are meant to suggest a standard quality of excellence, serving as models for the student's development of conscience and style, not as a sacred canon. They provide a more or less chronological basis for the perennial classroom dialogue out of which will emerge a structured pattern of ideas. Although, for example, the seventh grader is not expected to read *Utopia* with more than a simple descriptive understanding of More's social concepts, his incipient understanding will bear cumulative fruit as he considers in his next year, again descriptively, Churchill's account of the great British and U.S. experiments in democracy, and later, when he builds in progressively more complex forms on More and Churchill to trace the development of political institutions throughout Western civilization. Whatever basic ideas are planted will be regularly watered and eventually harvested because every teacher knows the life-cycle of the entire curriculum.

As pertains to the old books, their dialogue with one another is also cumulative in time. The classical authors, schooled in a two-thousand-year-old tradition, addressed themselves as much to the past as to their contemporaries. They were not about to forego the enormous momentum of their intellectual and spiritual tradition unless, like Descartes, they hoped to correct a primal fault in it. Yet even Descartes' bold departure was illuminated by the whole tradition, as one aspect of a dialectical contradiction, when he established the countertradition that is at once the material blessing and spiritual curse of our age. We are, to be sure, caught in the struggle between the humanist-Christian tradition and its Cartesian-Baconian rival. Our humanity, our self-awareness, and our society's salvation depend on our ability to keep this dialectic alive and to find ourselves in it, neither of which is possible without first understanding the spokesmen for these warring traditions.

IV

Paideia, as the word denotes, blurs the distinction between knowing and doing, between the educated and the cultured man. Knowing not only derives from doing, as Aristotle and Dewey assert, but knowledge entails an obligation to act independently and creatively. Being learned is not enough. Man's learning must bind him to act in accordance with what he knows and impel him to participate in the whole culture by supporting or opposing its attributes. The paideutic man possesses an artistic temperament: he or she discriminates, and he or she creates. He judges experience according to its immanent beauty and truthfulness — its power to evoke a sense of style and of conscience in himself and in others. His keen sensibilities penetrate the veil of experience, and beyond that veil, he lays up his incorruptible riches.

The paideutic man's attitude toward such activities as painting, drawing, violin playing, dancing, and acting is amateurish, not professional. He knows that one cannot learn the culture defined by these activities passively. Since culture is the unique property of the participant, not of the spectator, the classical academy resists the modern tendency to select only the most talented for participating. The modern school, to the contrary, frequently regards culture as entertainment, and the educator's cultural mission is taken up with exposing his students to an assortment of entertainments. He hopes to arouse their uncritical appreciation of art without attempting to sharpen their habits of discrimination or to develop their participatory skills.

Prevailing methods of analysis do not teach students to discriminate between the good and the bad, the beautiful and the ugly, or the restorative and the destructive in art. Under the eye of analysis, all art is equal and all forms of "culture" are affirmed, the football game and the opera, the ballet and the discotheque. Here again, we see the modern school pandering to the *demos* rather than working to sustain the normative tensions demanded by its dialectical role in a democratic society. To make matters worse, whenever an exception is made to the general rule against participatory culture and a student receives instruction in singing or dancing or painting, the approach and rationale are decidedly professional. The student is encouraged to regard himself as a glamourous performer, with a rich and admiring audience. His avaricious and burning ego consumes the transcendent value of the art.

If the modern school values culture at all, it does so for strictly social or political reasons; the individual and religious dimensions of a student's cultural needs it overlooks. Because it has methodically excluded the study of man's individual and religious domains, it cannot meet his cultural needs for aesthetic and moral discernment, or for the discipline and opportunity to acquire a wide range of participatory skills. What is the value of art as a simple act of self-expression or of worship if the school ignores man's individual and religious domains? Why should a student, lacking the intention or ability to become a Segovia, wish to master the classical guitar? Why should he squander hours on painstaking practice without the expectation of social acclaim or monetary reward, especially when the pleasure of listening to a Vivaldi concerto can be had simply by putting a record on the stereo? Ultimately, what is the utility of expending state monies and teachers' energies on students with limited artistic abilities and amateurish ambitions?

But the classical academy, intent on educating each individual for an abundant, responsible life in all his domains, grants to the arts individual and religious value in addition to the social and political. *Paideia* defines civilization not as a collection of art objects or political institutions or cultural happenings, but as the average man's level of participation in the affairs of art, literature, worship, invention, and polity. Classical education rebukes the modern man who glories in the Parthenon as a work of rare genius, while failing to identify that genius with average men embodying the spirit of *paideia* or to draw the obvious conclusion as regards modern education and its analytical, utilitarian bias. Blinded by the scientific myth of a one-dimensional man, modern man cannot recognize the integral value of the arts to his dying individual and religious domains.

The proposal for a classical curriculum makes obligatory each student's constant participation in both the fine and performing arts. In the performing arts, the student is offered a choice among choral music, instrumental music/ orchestra, drama, or dance. The curriculum proposal incorporates the performing arts for more than philosophical reasons, however. As part of the unified curriculum, the performing arts are assured adequate rehearsal time and facilities without scheduling conflicts, while the demands on students' time outside the regular school day are reduced, and evenings are free for reading and relaxation. The classical academy's performing arts program guarantees a place for every student, regardless of his ability or previous experience. In addition, its program complements, wherever reasonable, the work of the school of humane letters, so that from time to time Period 9 or the Assembly Period can be set aside for performing arts presentations that have bearing on the students' work in humane letters. A choral group might prepare a brief program of Ambrosian and Gregorian chants for the seventh or tenth graders, or a scene from Wilde's *The Importance of Being Ernest* might be enacted before the eleventh graders.

Neither are the fine arts offered on a take-it-or-leave-it basis in the school of arts and languages. "I don't like art," or "My child is not creative," or "Art is not practical" — how often have we heard these attacks on art education! Yet the inability to find pleasure in great art is all the more reason to study it, not to be excused from the art class; whereas an apparent lack of creativity — whatever that means — will certainly not be corrected by forfeiting the opportunity to gain some artistic knowledge and discipline, both necessary grounds, although not guarantees, of creativity. Without knowledge and discipline, the aspiring artist ends up repeating himself and the past unconsciously, and his art passes swiftly from the egoistic level of self-expression and therapy to the substratum of neuroticism and despair. As for the practicality of art, it is probably true that the study of art is no more essential than the civilization that it sustains (and which makes both work and leisure possible and potentially meaningful). The fine arts, therefore, are taught in a series of academic and studio art projects that complement the work in the school of humane letters, integrating instruction in the elements, principles, and techniques of art with historical and literary content. This approach does not put at unfair advantage those with special creative gifts, nor does it harm those without these gifts to become acquainted in a rigorous manner with the rich tradition in art and with the development of its manifold concepts, personalities, and techniques.

Below is a list of seven fine arts projects to illustrate what might be used to complement, in this instance, the seventh grade's study of medieval Britain in the school of humane letters:

1. Architecture: Hadrian's Wall; Roman baths, fortifications and country villas; monastery at Iona; Norman churches; medieval London; and so forth:
   a. Drawings: the use of perspective
   b. Three-dimensional model building using illustration board
   c. Floor plans, elevations, and city planning
2. Basic design: Celtic cross:
   a. Black and white design in cut paper, reverse, mirror image, negative space
   b. Rubbings
   c. Wood cuts
3. Bayeaux tapestry:
   a. Stitchery appliqué
   b. Weaving
   c. Figure studies concentrating on narrative and action
4. Basic design: medieval banners and escutcheons:
   a. Stencil designs
   b. Painted
   c. Batik
   d. Stitchery and appliqué
5. Cartography: maps of conquest and pilgrimage:
   a. Drawings and paintings
   b. Print-making
   c. (Coordinated with Earth Science I)
6. Conceptual interpretation of Tolkien figures:
   a. Ceramic with low fire glazes
   b. Ink renderings (possibly using illustrative techniques)
   c. Linoleum reduction prints
7. Development of Christian liturgy – historical account using slides and reproductions:
   a. The Mass: its ritual and symbol
   b. The Mass: its music
   c. The Mass: its costumes and appurtenances
   d. (Coordinated with Performing Arts)

V

The school of maths and sciences begins in grade 7 with a course in pre-algebra and a two-year course in earth science. The study of algebra naturally depends upon the student's mastery of arithmetic, and it is grounded on one fundamental assumption: that an understanding of mathematical principles and of the reasoning behind each step in the solution of problems is infinitely more important than the ability to assign correct answers to problems. The foundation laid in the beginning will determine how far the student will go in his study of mathematics, how adroitly he will apply mathematical reasoning in other disciplines, how quickly he will gain an intuitive second sense into the nature of numbers and their functions, and most importantly, how deeply he will delight in the science of numbers. For these reasons, often the best teacher ought to be assigned to students at this level. If a solid foundation is not laid in the seventh and eighth grades, the student will grow frustrated and bored with his mathematical studies, and the faulty foundation will have to be relaid. Relaying the foundation is time consuming and not always possible, however, since once a student learns a mathematical process incorrectly, any attempt to reteach the process often breeds confusion rather than clarity.

The chief sin of the modern school in this regard springs from a pervasive attitude in the teaching profession — a peculiar scorn for the basic ideas, underlying assumptions, and fundamental skills of *paideia* and a consequent desire to teach literature, not literacy; creativity, not discipline; answers, not questions; solutions, not methods. This attitude, which may appear to foster impressive learning at an early age, severely limits the student's later intellectual growth, regardless of the superior instruction he is expected to receive at higher levels. Since the difficulty of teaching the fundamentals of a subject to young minds approaching it for the first time is perhaps the severest test of one's teaching ability, requiring a profound and clear insight into the nature of the subject, one must question the sincerity of teachers as teachers who eschew this level of instruction. Moreover, an inadequate teacher in the seventh grade poisons the well of learning at its source, whereas later, his misinstruction would simply be unfortunate and might even benefit a few talented students by introducing early into their mathematical studies a forensic element. (Few things are more instructive than an honest disagreement with the teacher.)

The traditional view of mathematics as an excellent discipline for the mind has suffered much criticism of late, as has what was assumed to be the possibility of transferring mathematical processes to other areas of thought and endeavor. It is difficult to argue on this score, as on many others, before all the diverse results of psychological experiment and sociological research are in. While waiting for the induction to end, however, we might profitably reconsider the really rather modest claims of the classical tradition. The study of mathematics, the ancients believed, reinforces the mind's powers of concentration, memory, and logical process. As anyone who has solved a system of equations to find three unknowns realizes, he has had to exercise these three powers: dispelling from the mind all that is extraneous to the problem, recalling those methods and techniques pertinent to the solution, and working through the problem in a logical sequence. The cumulative and coherent study of mathematics is, in fact, a microcosm of the entire curriculum and reflects in its expanding field the workings of the scholarly mind in a manner analogous to that which we examined in the field of arts and letters. The purpose of concentration is to draw uninterruptedly upon memory in order to make logical connections.

Nor should the psychologically ambiguous but commonsensical idea of a "mental discipline" confuse anyone. Admittedly, to some, it conjures up the picture of a little muscle behind the ears grown to gigantic proportions having solved a thousand quadratic equations, but the discipline of mathematics is not of that sort at all. It is a habit of mind subjugating the young person's natural inclination toward intellectual sloth and self-centeredness; it teaches him to delight in making the scholarly discoveries that usually attend an organized search. It stands as a mighty bulwark against the heretical and preposterous notion that there can be sound learning without concentration, memory, and logical process. The modern attempt to introduce mathematics in a school environment that plays down these three powers of mind not only seems to validate the criticism of mathematics as a useless mental discipline, but it subverts the scholarly habits essential to a student's enjoyment and success in the study of numbers. Where these habits are ignored, an early flowering can only be bought at the price of shallow roots.

VI

The relationship between mathematics and science in the classical academy can be described as one of coordination, not integration. Both mathematicians and scientists ought to be aware of what the other is doing so that the mathematician can, where appropriate, illustrate his principles from science, and the scientist can, when he wishes to, demonstrate his observations and experimental results mathematically. But total integration of the two would violate the logical internal development of each, retarding their teaching, while implying to the student a *necessary* connection between the symbolic language of numbers and the material universe. Although this connection is compellingly drawn by modern science and must be thoroughly explored by the advanced scholar, the secondary school student's mathematical curiosity should not be bound by the rule of material applicability, for there is a beauty in numbers, perhaps a mystery, suggesting the ideal and touching the transcendent. This awesome sense — as testified to by all those who have labored at the distant frontiers of both mathematics and sciences — should never be sacrificed in early learning for the purpose of making mathematics the scullery maid of the technological sciences.

The two-year course in earth science allows the younger student whose mathematical skills are slight to approach the study of science as the ancients did. They looked around themselves at the earth they inhabited and asked: Where is the earth? Does the sky move? What causes the wind to blow? Why does it rain? How are clouds formed? What is the value of rain to man, and what does it teach him about himself and his life on earth? Of these six questions, we today are least likely to ask the last, whereas the ancients usually hastened through the first five to afford themselves the leisure to cogitate upon the sixth. From this question, they culled their wisdom — that arrestingly exact, simple statement revealing man to himself through the material universe. "Love your enemies, bless them that curse you . . . that ye may be the children of your Father which is in heaven: for he maketh his sun to rise on the evil and on the good, and sendeth rain on the just and on the unjust."

The Greeks changed this emphasis, but never dropped the last question. Nor should the classical academy. The absence of this question from our scientific inquiries today is neither natural to our humanity nor beneficial to our understanding of the material universe. Where knowledge grows without wisdom and without reverence, it threatens both our humanity and our world. Yet modern man suppresses his natural desire to throw himself in the path of science and ask his baffling normative questions (baffling to science, but not insignificant to man). Scientific technology, acting like an opiate, calms his normative inquisitiveness with the hype of its gadgetry's comfort and security and with the fusion-promise of technological answers to all foreseeable problems. This opiate, like all opiates, destroys man's critical faculties and makes him blind to the fact that the technological "fix" hides its evil consequences by taking a position of moral aloofness while "pushing" the practical value of its narcotic. Science must be pulled down from its nonnormative pedestal. The penetrating intensity of its analysis must be used to expose the narcotic effects of technological advancement on man and on his inquisitiveness.

The classical science teacher constantly asks himself: "How does this or that scientific truth touch my students' lives and increase their understanding of themselves and of their purposes?" A resolution of values must attend the study of science, and analysis must be framed within the normative inquiry if science is to serve life, not destroy it. Quantification and analysis are the experts, not the policy makers; they are meant to wait upon, not define, the human utility function. Every scientific truth must be examined in the light of its human utility function. Although *paideia* is accomplished in means, its chief objective is the definition of ends, the articulation of human utility functions — an objective not compromised by an exclusive reliance upon the analytical methods of the scientific means. The science of *paideia* reflects this un-modern emphasis, commencing with a study of the earth that innoculates the young student with a critical, normative view of the physics, chemistry, and biology to follow.

A second year of biology concludes the science requirement of the classical curriculum because of the philosophical sophistication of the normative issues it raises. Of course, physics and chemistry also raise perplexing moral questions, but the great normative debate has moved in the last decade from physics to biology and promises to reside there for some time. Not only has the technical complexity of biology mushroomed, but the fundamental moral and social implications of biological research — whether predicated on theories like evolutionism and behavioralism or premised upon microelectronic discoveries, like those of endorphin and the enkephalins — threaten to burst on our children in all their domains — the individual, the social and political, and the religious. It is crucial that *paideia* form in our young a dynamic normative core able to withstand morally and intellectually the shock of scientific revolutions. No one need fear the proliferation of scientific discoveries in a society bent on moral ends and in normative control of its technological destinies. In such a society, the normative does not tether but merely bridles the analytical.

12

THE SCHOOL WITHIN THE SCHOOL

To render the discipline by influence effectual, it is
necessary that the character of each student be thoroughly
understood, and that their confidence and affection
should be secured. These objects are here attained in this
way. When a class enters college, it is divided into two
parts, and each division is put under the charge of a
Tutor. He generally continues with them three years, if
he remains in office so long. He is the Tutor not of a
language or of a science, but of a class, or a division. He
meets them three times a day. He becomes thoroughly
acquainted with their characters. He speaks of them as
his; and considers himself as in a degree responsible for
their good conduct. A mutual attachment is formed
between them. He gains from them an affectionate
confidence; which could hardly be expected, where each
student has a half a dozen different instructors; and
each instructor half a dozen different sets of pupils, in
the course of a week. It is principally through the Tutors,
that the Faculty influence the students.

—Jeremiah Day (President of Yale University)

I

No reform of education is possible so long as teachers remain captive within
their present school environments. The greatest single constraint on school
reform, especially reform that reemphasizes the role of the teacher, is the difficulty in obtaining teachers whose expectations and abilities coincide with the
reforming vision. The expectations and abilities of many teachers are flawed
from the beginning, owing to a shallow or narrow education that either ended
in college or continued sporadically at schools of education, where they
attended classes in child psychology and in teaching technology. For others,

147

the years of routine, of declining standards, and of institutional disintegration have worn away their early idealism, while devaluing the currency of their ability. For all, the institutional disorder, fragmentation, and incoherence of the modern school breed only an instinct to survive, not the ability to think and teach creatively and courageously.

Keefer, in Herman Wouk's *The Caine Mutiny* (1951), speaks for any number of contemporary institutions, including the school, when he describes the navy as "all child's play. The work has been fragmentized by a few excellent brains at the top, on the assumption that near-morons will be responsible for each fragment." Modern organizations, keen on exorcising the unpredictable human element, favor an institutional structure designed to accommodate the weakest element, in which no one person's negligence or incompetence can prevent the whole organization from accomplishing its goals. No presumptuous faith in champions here — no Davids or Hectors in this system! Modern organizational practice is not predicated upon making people better than what they are, but it accepts them for what they are — or for something worse. The system built to accommodate near-morons, however, makes near-morons of everyone in the system, but this is not thought too great a price to pay for ensuring the achievement of the organization's goals.

Nonetheless, the problem of motivation eventually overtakes the moron-proof organization. Whereas at the present level of individual incompetency, its goals may seem assured, there is no guarantee that without demanding more of its people, the organization can maintain the present level and continue to meet its goals. There are gradations, after all, even among morons; and the system built to accommodate near-morons will, when left to its own devices, turn near-morons into utter vegetables. Hence, the organization must find a way of motivating its people and of vitiating the reductionist logic of its system. In this paradox, the modern organization is trapped and at odds with itself: it is designed to avoid the interruption of its goals by morons, but because its design also induces moronic behavior, it must devise schemes for motivating the near-morons in the organization to perform consistently at — but not too far above — their level of incompetency.

Thus is the modern school organized to ensure that the teacher, as represented by the least competent member of his calling, is not in a position to do significant damage to the student or to interfere with the school's "educational" goals. The teacher's classes are large; his relation with the students, formal and fleeting. If reputed to be weak in his field, the teacher is obliged to teach the fundamental ideas and skills of his discipline to the younger students on the assumption that there he does the least harm. No student need be exposed to him more than five hours a week, and then, only in one discrete subject area. The teacher is not challenged to perform more than the simple task for which he was prepared years ago in college or normal school, and that task he performs repeatedly, if not mechanically. In summary, the chance for a teacher to exert for good (or for bad) a serious influence on his students is organizationally proscribed. Moreover, since there are no established means for constantly challenging and enlarging the thoughts and skills of the teacher within the school itself, any suggestion of basic reform poses a personal, as well as professional, threat to him.

Now, such a moron-proof organization may make good sense for the navy or even for General Motors, neither of which exist to fashion a human product, but for the school, this practice is an outrage. How can the "educational" goals of a school take precedence over the development of the individual teacher and student when the formation of *paideia* in the individual *is* its educational goal? Certainly, it is worth risking the dubious influence of an incompetent teacher here and there if a profound and intimate teacher-pupil relationship is our best chance to accomplish this goal. The attempt to apply general theories of management and of organization to the school ignores the unique character of education and of the school's peculiarly dialectical methods. The school must educate all of its denizens if it is to educate any of them; all must give repeated testimony to their active involvement in the learning dialogue. Education consists not in accepting the student's or the teacher's level of ability, but in challenging it; not in reflecting the expectations of society, but in questioning them.

The challenging of teachers and students, as well as the questioning of society, ought to be part of the organizational design of the school, even at the risk of making the school an uncomfortable place for the individual who resists committing himself to the perpetual quest for knowledge. For this reason, there exists a Teachers' Seminar within the school of humane letters. This seminar meets regularly by grade once or twice a week. Ideally, teachers from the School of Maths and Sciences and from the School of Arts and Languages should also be a part of the Teachers' Seminar because their disciplines always have a bearing, of one sort or another, on the current subject of study in the humane letters.

II

The Teachers' Seminar has many uses. Primarily, it offers teachers an opportunity to discuss the current readings on the humane letters syllabus, drawing on one another's academic backgrounds and individual insights. The seminar may discuss pedagogical approaches to a specific reading or decide to substitute a new reading for an old one that has proven ineffective. Although the readings suggested in the curriculum proposal can be discussed at depths that would stimulate even the most erudite scholar, it is important that the teacher emerge from the seminar with a clear notion of what the normative implications and consequences of the book in question are, of how the book fits into his students' pattern of study, and of how he and his colleagues intend to provoke their students to ask the critical questions.

Second, the teacher's past analytical training within a restricted subject area requires that the seminar reeducate him to serve effectively the classical academy's normative purposes. The teacher must learn how to draw the connection between life and learning by couching the rigorous requirements of his analysis within a normative inquiry. He hounds the scent of an idea wherever it leads, never afraid to admit ignorance, but never happy to rest in it. He uses his mastery of one discipline as a springboard into other disciplines. The sincerity of his search and the integrity of his methods inspire his colleagues and spread contagiously to his students. Indeed, in the seminar, the teacher is inspired, judged, and challenged to be better than he is. In the seminar, the teacher learns as he helps to define the purposes of the classical academy. In the seminar, the teacher is evaluated personally, constructively, and spontaneously. The seminar becomes the living heart of the *paideia*.

Third, the seminar prepares study and essay questions for each week's reading. The weekly essay question in particular is meant to ferret out the essential argument in the reading. Usually centering around some controversial point, a matter of judgment rather than of fact, the question demands that the student narrow the field to avoid ambiguity, define his terms, and take a stand that he proceeds to defend from the text. The questions should challenge but not frustrate the student, help him to separate the significant from the obvious, and lure him into a personal involvement with the subject on some occasions, while asking him to defend an unpopular thesis on others. They should encourage the student to draw on his previous study for comparisons between writers, epochs, and ideas. In this regard, one of the chief tasks of the seminar is to coordinate the questioning in humane letters with other aspects of the curriculum and to enhance the teacher's awareness of the relationship between the current reading and its curricular cousins.

The weekly essay ought to be carefully graded, with rivers of red ink running down the margins, and reviewed personally with each student at the time it is handed back. A compelling reason for having small classes meeting frequently is to allow the teacher to assign and grade more writing both in and out of class, as well as to return writing promptly and personally. Since each class meets at least twice a day, not every class should follow the same format. Many may be reserved for directed study (*travaux practiques*), with the teacher on hand to give individual tutelage or to return written work in personal conferences.

In the early grades, most instruction in grammar should be meted out in the context of individual writing conferences, so that class-time is not consumed with abstract grammatical drill. When drill became unfashionable in the 1960s, many schools decided to abandon instruction in grammar altogether; but declining verbal abilities and writing skills are giving educational analysts second thoughts. A return to drill, however, is not the answer. Drill cannot bridge the wide gap between the student who needs grammar to strengthen his verbal abilities and the student who, often because of a literary heritage in the home, does not. Nor can drill alone make the essential connection between good grammar and a student's written and spoken solecisms. It seems preferable, therefore, to make grammatical instruction a largely individual matter, based directly on the student's own writing and speaking, although this ideal can seldom be realized because of the way most schools are impersonally structured.

Unlike the weekly essay question, the study questions do not necessarily entail any written work. The study questions provide the student with critical tools for unearthing the author's major concerns by focusing a student's attention while he reads. The wrongheaded custom of many teachers to wait until after their students have read a book before questioning them on it does nothing to remedy the passive reading habits of a television-reared generation, and it puts a false premium on random retention and recall. Consequently, students forget or fall asleep over what they read unless the plot can offer them the superficial thrills of a roller coaster ride, and the teacher fritters away hours of class-time trying to call forth a recollection with questions that stroke sensibilities but seldom enliven intelligence. Discussions center around what the reading says rather than on what it means or on how the student feels about what it says rather than on why he feels that way. In the end, the student is evaluated on his ability to remember, but not to think. Study questions, on the contrary, press the student to attack his reading critically. They direct his note taking, furnish a basis for classroom discussion, and eventually provide him with a comprehensive means of reviewing for examinations. They facilitate the workings of a scholarly mind by suggesting where connections can be made, and most important, they stamp each student with an aggressive reading habit and a relentlessly critical habit of mind.

III

The Teachers' Seminar also determines how to advance the development of the basic skills, concepts, and themes of *paideia*. The nature of freedom, for instance, is a recurring problem in *paideia*; every year, various readings in the humane letters' syllabus address it. Jewish, Greek, Roman, and Christian concepts of freedom differ. How? Why? How have these differences influenced our modern attitudes toward freedom? How have changing concepts of freedom influenced the historical development of political institutions, social institutions, and religious institutions? What is the connection between freedom and morality, freedom and authority, freedom and the law, and freedom and responsibility? These are not the sort of questions that one asks casually to a seventh grader, but they ought to kindle ideas with which every twelfth grader is familiar and conversant, because over the years, their teachers have persistently raised questions touching on these ideas. As ninth graders, they were asked to define the influence of monotheism and the worship of Yahweh on the early Hebrew concept of freedom and of government. As tenth graders, they wrote essays contrasting Greek political idealism with Roman pragmatism or discussing the threat of early Christian doctrine to Roman political authority. Perhaps they debated the relative merits of the positive Hebrew concept of law as opposed to the negative Roman concept. In short, the Teachers' Seminar, conscious of what the students have examined and have yet to examine, shapes questions befitting the students' ongoing and deepening investigation into those normative currents that sweep the human soul along.

By dismissing the past or by giving it only cursory textbook treatment, modern education produces students whom T. S. Eliot (1974) called "provincials of time." These students regard the past with ignorant condescension, assuming that all its scant benefits, through some mysterious process of progressive evolution, have been retained, while its evils have for the most part been shed away. They are infected with the fever of progress, supposing that the mere passage of time acts like a great threshing machine, discarding the chaff and preserving the wheat. Whatever kernels of truth this world ever possessed are somewhere in the loaf now being proffered by science. Nor, in this condition, can the young stomach the medicine of the past, with its stern warnings and meticulous instructions for human improvement printed on the label. In a school predicated only upon science, the student can be nothing more than what he is. That, to be sure, can be developed – and human development results from yielding to certain inner patterns of truth (to which only the psychiatrist is privy), not from imposing the crushing obligations of a historical dogma or of an Ideal Type. The student is not asked to bear any responsibility for a past from which he is intellectually and existentially cut off.

Perhaps his notion of freedom demands that the student remain a cutoff, conscienceless "provincial of time"; but aside from the repetitive folly of such a notion, as popularly prophesied by Santayana, the real danger in this attitude is that it takes refuge in technological analogy and refuses to accept the possibility of losing the vital effects of a rich heritage that cannot simply be written down and stored in museums and libraries, but must be learned and acted upon in order to preserve and to benefit humanity. The knowledge of how men live and of how they ought to live is inseparable and has ancient roots: not all of its finest flowerings are contemporary. This knowledge, the true knowledge of *paideia*, requires a discerning appreciation for the past, unprejudiced by an assumption of progress or regress. Although analysis alone winks at such assumptions and thereby plays into the hands of any ideology professing a privileged insight into these matters, the classical academy, with its normative emphasis, studies the past with an eye for calling such assumptions into question.

Because of its chronological approach to subject matter, the school of humane letters will be guilty of producing "provincials of time" if it teaches the arts and letters with an explicit or implicit assumption of progress. The Teachers' Seminar must root out this assumption, therefore, by distinguishing between dialectical and synthetic questions. Dialectical questions address the recurring tensions and controversies in man's thought and condition; these are questions of war and peace, freedom and authority, faith and doubt, reason and emotion, knowledge and uncertainty, motivation and behavior, morality and realpolitik, idealism and pragmatism, and so forth. The resolution of these tensions clearly has nothing to do with the mere passage of time, as the great literature of all ages reminds us; but a wise resolution in the present day is crucial to the individual, to the school, and to society at large. In most instances, resolutions cannot be made by the few for the many: salvation must come to every person as an individual.

Synthetic questions, on the other hand, trace patterns of growth or disintegration: the rise of the nation-state concept, for example, or the gradual disappearance of tribal taboos and primitive mores. By their nature, synthetic questions are vulnerable to hidden presuppositions, for any two different persons may see the same series of events as progressive and regressive, radical and reactionary, salutary and deleterious. To leave synthetic questions in the blind hands of analysis, where normative presuppositions pass undetected, constitutes a distortion of knowledge and a great danger to sound learning. The Teachers' Seminar must remove this danger by framing questions that examine, say, the validity of the nation-state concept in the modern era or the value in hypothetically resurrecting certain primitive mores. Few discussions of synthetic ideas are innocent of an attitude toward the subject. By identifying this attitude and calling it into question, the teacher prevents his students from reading a false progress automatically into history, while urging them to adopt a normative attitude of their own that they can defend and live by.

Also, the school of humane letters avoids the presumption of progress by studying arts and letters within a first-hand historical context. Allowing the past to speak through old books directly to the student flattens time and defeats the progressive implications of a textbook's chronological approach to subject matter. The decisive lesson of any first-hand study of history is that for almost every modern thought or innovation, there exists an historical precedent illuminating and sometimes outshining it. The essay and study questions prepared by the Teachers' Seminar ought to ensure the historical inviolability of each work of art and fiction, while provoking the student to identify the past's hold on the present moment.

IV

Besides reeducating the teacher to serve the classical academy's normative purposes, the seminar performs several practical, administrative functions. These include arranging the schedule for lectures, assemblies, debates, and examinations, as well as writing and grading examinations. At the end of each semester, the seminar, acting as a committee of external examiners, writes one standard examination for all students in its respective grade, and it marks this examination without regard to which student belongs to which teacher. The individual student's teacher will of course return and comment personally on the examination, and he may appeal the grade to the committee if he wishes to. In addition, a test in grammar is given at the conclusion of the seventh, eighth, and ninth-grade years, and during these years, the out-of-class projects are handled at the discretion of the Teachers' Seminar for each form. Tenth and eleventh graders have specific research papers due in the spring to their respective

Teachers' Seminars, while seniors are free to reflect on their *paideia* in the Problems of Knowledge class.

The Teachers' Seminar regularly schedules interclass debates based on a controversial topic. This topic may come from a single reading on the syllabus, or it may require some additional research, or it may integrate previously studied works in response to a recurring thematic controversy — for example, resolved: that preparation for war increases the chances for peace; resolved: that Christ is a Greek philosopher, not a Hebrew God; resolved: that democracy is the cradle of tyranny; or resolved: that all heroes are scoundrels and knaves. Every student is expected to prepare and to participate in these debates.

Debate is a natural vehicle for achieving the goals of the classical academy: the cultivation of the conscience and style of a learned, graceful, inquisitive, just, self-aware world-citizen. Debate teaches not only the felicities of speech, but an intellectual courtesy and honesty, as well as a poise and confidence in address that splendidly dramatize the union between the idea and the deed. To plead the case of an idea persuasively forces the advocate to make the idea his own — to feel it, to glory in it, as well as to understand its critical strengths and weaknesses. Ideas, thus accepted as dogma and invigorated by debate, take on a life of their own within the mind of the student.

This universal forensic activity is the special mark of the classical academy wherein the arbitrary and often exclusionary distinction between the curricular and the extracurricular is abandoned (debate is woven into the curriculum), and all activities are for everyone and each activity promotes the normative purposes of the whole academy (debate is not reserved for the aspiring lawyers and club joiners). To be sure, this harmony rewards the loss of a certain eclecticism and freedom of parts, but the academy's singularly idiosyncratic, intimate, and moral purposes demand no less. Unlike the democratic state that generates our students' opinions and conditions their parents' expectations, the classical academy does not derive its concept of the best from the will of the majority. It does not exist to accept the status quo in society or in the individual, but to challenge and transform it. Its true method is not compromise, but unyielding pursuit of an idea of perfection. The Teachers' Seminar, a school within the school, safeguards, nurtures, and articulates this idea of perfection in its careful selection of readings and in its constant improvement and evaluation of the essay, study, and debate questions, as well as of the work of teachers and students.

EPILOGUE

Let knowledge grow from more to more,
But more of reverence in us dwell.

—Alfred Lord Tennyson

I

Modern criticism of general education focuses mostly on the symptoms of the school's declining academic standards. A mushrooming elective system, grade inflation, narrow specialization, open admissions, pass-fail options, minority programs and quotas, "relevant" learning, student curriculum committees — if only the abuses attending these innovations could be remedied, the critics suggest, standards of learning would once again rise on the road "back to basics." At the moment, this is a fashionable sentiment. Even Harvard has updated its "Redbook" in accordance with the new trend in criticism. But how often has treating symptoms produced an effective cure? In fact, our modern educational establishment is expert at treating symptoms, at describing a disease exactly with its marvelous tools of analysis, while ignoring the invisible causes. The analytical-minded school administrator has been so long thinking in terms of the school's battered public image that whenever a flaw appears in its image, he instinctively rushes to the cosmetic case for a cure. But the reality behind the image has changed, and administrative cosmetics are no more salubrious than Band-Aids on bullet holes.

While the modern school was looking to its image with cosmetic innovations, many of which are now wearing off, the underlying reality of education in the United States was slowly changing. We have examined in this book two complementary characteristics of this change: the impact of science and technology on our methods of instruction and society's new attitude toward the value of learning. Science and technology demand an objective, detached, analytical

155

approach to learning in opposition to the involved, personal, normative ways of a classical education. There is no danger in this, however, until science's method of analysis begins to control all avenues of human inquiry, as it does today. Then knowledge becomes atomized and man, politicized, his quest for knowledge excluding him ex hypothesi from his vast individual and religious domains.

Nor is this all. Science's analytical methods and positivist presuppositions restrict the questions we ask in education and about education, and we begin mouthing a catechism of questions for which our techniques can provide answers, whether the answers are significant or not. In education, this preoccupation with false or trivial questions makes the student adept at "faking it," that is, at finding the right answers to the wrong questions, questions he has never really asked himself, questions without normative consequence or implication. In this way, the prevailing analytical methods of instruction separate knowledge from responsibility and learning from life, a break that we vainly endeavor to patch up by calling for an education of utility. This call inspires society's new attitude toward the value of learning.

Americans no longer expect education to form the child after an ideal image or to develop a refined sense of conscience and style in the young person. To speak nowadays of education's formative role in the life of virtue or of learning's transcendent value is sure to invite smiles, or sneers, and not a little mystification. Who dares to suggest that we spend tax dollars on the risky investment of forming virtuous and wise young people? The benefits flowing from such an investment, perhaps because they are neither directly political nor economic, are no longer obvious — although in an era of rising crime and social neuroses and of declining courtesy and social cohesion, they ought to be.

The modern school is not blameless in regard to society's new attitude toward the value of learning. Education's complacent private sector has persistently been represented to the American public as a means of achieving social and economic superiority, while the galumphing public sector builds upon the utilitarian rationale, making education a yellow-brick road to social and economic equality, by which it too means superiority. To keep their promises, both sectors have had to shelve their ideals, their uncompromising vision of a more perfect person in a more perfect society and their belief that this vision can become a reality through the pursuit of knowledge. Lacking this vision, the modern school knows no better than to cater to the very utilitarian expectations it helped to create. Like mindless Pinocchio who fell in with the fox and the cat, the school without this vision falls under the utilitarian influences of the marketplace and the state.

Both state and marketplace accelerate the trend toward utilitarian learning that in turn encourages a cosmetic approach to reform. The typical criticism leveled at the school by business and government is: you have not taught the young to *do* anything. Contrary to Aristotle, who wanted education to teach the young how to use their leisure for reaching the full stature of their humanity and how to realize their greatest happiness in the life of virtue, business and government view education as a preparation for work and an indoctrination into the practical life via the enticements of the life of pleasure. The modern educator accommodates by adding vocational courses to the curriculum or by requiring more classes in composition: it is a simple matter of determining what skills are *presently* in demand.

But ironically, the young can do nothing because as the effort intensifies to prepare them for the practical life, they are not learning the rudiments of thinking in terms of the essential dialectic that we have discussed. The young are not learning to ask important questions, for the normative questions opening up a life of virtue are methodically barred from the classroom. Nor are they getting a chance to discover the wonderful connection between life and learning because their utilitarian instructors ignore their major human concerns. By the time the average student leaves high school, he is indisposed to the responsible learning of *paideia*; he cannot recognize his need for an inner change, a *morphosis*; nor is he fired with a passion to be made better by what he studies. The average student has been given no mythology on which to build his or her life other than a glut of movies and television dramas and no ideal models other than a cult of rock and sports idols. He has failed to develop the habits of mind necessary for further learning: concentration, inquisitiveness, intuition, memory, logical process, and industry; he lacks the talent to ask general questions or to grasp the general principle common to a set of disparate ideas or situations. Above all, he wants character: the ability, according to Aristotle, to make a wise choice when that choice is not obvious.

True learning is revealed in character; it is not a matter of courses or degrees or preparation for a job. "Education," wrote John Ruskin (1968), "does not mean teaching people to know what they do not know; it means teaching them to behave as they do not behave." True learning induces a patient, inquiring, ruminative, and good-humored disposition. When good humor deserts the educated man, his good manners sustain him. True learning begins in dogma and ends in dialectic. "It is an experiment that is not independent of the one who experiments" (Mueller 1965). True learning is normative: it measures what is against what ought to be. It asks why, as well as why not.

True learning makes affirmation and acknowledges limitation; it begets honesty and humility, compassion toward man and reverence toward God. The educated man is never aggressive in his behavior or arrogant in his mood: these are marks of an ignoramus, or of the modern student, with a talent for "faking it." True learning brings man to a full stature of humanity in all his domains — the individual, the social and political, and the religious. True learning possesses the confidence and good conscience that come from acting in accordance with one's knowledge of the truth. True learning knows what is good, serves it above self, reproduces it, and recognizes that in knowledge lies this responsibility. True learning resolves the paradox between educating for the world's fight and for the soul's salvation in favor of the active life of virtue. Only a saved soul can fight the world's fight and know the cost of losing and the value of what it has won.

BIBLIOGRAPHY

Aquinas, Thomas. *The Summa Theologica*. Chicago: Encyclopedia Britannica, 1955.

Archambault, Reginald D. *John Dewey on Education*. New York: Random House, 1964.

Arendt, Hannah. *The Life of the Mind*. New York: Harcourt Brace Jovanovich, 1978.

Aristotle. *Eudemian Ethics*. Edited by H. Rackham. London: Heinemann, 1961.

_____. *Nicomachean Ethics*. Edited by H. Rackham. London: Heinemann, 1975.

_____. *Parts of Animals*. Edited by A.L. Peck. London: Heinemann, 1961.

_____. *The Poetics*. Edited by W. Rhys Roberts, London: Heinemann, 1927.

_____. *Politics*. Edited by H. Rackham. London: Heinemann, 1959.

Auchincloss, Louis. *The Rector of Justin*. New York: Avon Books, 1964.

Bacon, Francis. *Advancement of Learning. Novum Organum. New Atlantis*. 1 vol. Chicago: Encyclopedia Britannica, 1955.

Baker, Carlos. *Selected Poetry and Prose of Shelley*. New York: Random House, 1951.

Barfield, Owen. *Saving the Appearances: A Study in Idolatry*. New York: Harcourt, Brace & World.

Barr, Stringfellow. *Voices That Endured*. Englewood Cliffs, N.J.: Prentice-Hall, 1971.

Bruner, Jerome. *The Process of Education.* Cambridge, Mass.: Harvard University Press, 1960.

_____. *Toward a Theory of Instruction.* Cambridge, Mass.: Harvard University Press, 1966.

Burnet, John. *The Ethics of Aristotle.* Saint Claire Shores, Mich.: Scholarly, 1976.

Chesterton, G.K. *The Everlasting Man.* New York: Dodd, Mead & Company, 1953.

Churchill, Winston. *The Birth of Britain.* New York: Dodd, Mead & Company, 1956.

Cohen, David K., and Garet, Michael S. "Reforming Educational Policy with Applied Social Research." *Harvard Educational Review* 45 (February 1975): 17-43.

Curtis, Charles P., and Greenslet, Ferris. *The Practical Cogitator.* New York: Dell, 1975.

Dante. *The Selected Works.* London: Chatto & Windus, 1972.

Durant, Will. *The Renaissance.* New York: Simon & Schuster, 1953.

Eliot, T.S. *The Family Reunion.* New York: Harcourt, Brace & World, 1939.

_____. *On Poetry and Poets.* New York: Farrar, Straus & Giroux, 1974.

Erasmus. *Education of a Christian Prince.* Edited by Lester K. Born. New York: Octagon, 1965.

Feuer, Lewis S. *Marx & Engels: Basic Writings on Politics & Philosophy.* Garden City, N.Y.: Doubleday, 1959.

Finley, M.I. *Knowledge of What?* The Encyclopedia Britannica Lecture. Edinburgh: University of Edinburgh, 1972.

Fitzgerald, Robert. *The Odyssey Homer.* New York: Doubleday, 1963.

Freud, Sigmund. *The Standard Edition of the Complete Psychological Works.* London: Hogarth, 1966-74.

Frye, Northrop. *Fearful Symmetry: A Study of William Blake.* Princeton, N.J.: Princeton University, 1974.

Gable, John Allen. "'He loved the Soaring Spirit of Man': The Life and Work of Hermann Hagedorn." *Theodore Roosevelt Association Journal* 3 (Fall 1977): 9-13.

Gaebelein, Frank E. *The Pattern of God's Truth*. Chicago: Moody, 1976.

Galen. *On the Natural Faculties*. Translated by A. J. Brock. London: Heinemann, 1952.

Gardner, John. *The Life and Times of Chaucer*. New York: Knopf, 1977.

Graves, Robert. *The Song of Songs*. New York: Clarkson N. Potter, 1973.

Halberstam, David. *The Best and the Brightest*. New York: Random House, 1972.

Haldane, Elizabeth S., and Ross, G.R.T. *The Philosophical Works of Descartes*. Cambridge: Cambridge University Press, 1969.

Harris, Marvin; Morgenbesser, Sidney; Rothschild, Joseph; and Wishy, Bernard. *Introduction to Contemporary Civilization in the West: A Source Book*. New York: Columbia University, 1960.

Herodotus. *The Histories*. Trans. by Aubrey de Sélincourt. Harmondsworth: Penguin Books, 1975.

Highet, Gilbert. *The Classical Tradition*. New York: Oxford University, 1971.

Huxley, Aldous. *The World of Aldous Huxley*. Edited by Charles J. Rolo. New York: Harper, 1947.

Isocrates. *Isocrates*. Vols. 1 and 2. Translated by George Norlin. London: Heinemann, 1956.

Jaeger, Werner. *Early Christianity and Greek Paideia*. Cambridge, Mass.: Harvard University Press, 1961.

James, William. *The Meaning of Truth*. Cambridge, Mass.: Harvard University Press, 1978.

Johnson, Samuel. *The Yale Edition of the Works of Samuel Johnson*. New Haven: Yale University, 1958.

Jowett, B. *The Dialogues of Plato*. Oxford: Clarendon, 1969.

Karp, Walter. "Textbook America." *Harper's*, May 1980, pp. 80-88.

King James Version of the Bible.

Livingston, Sir Richard. *Some Tasks for Education.* Bombay: Oxford University, 1950.

Livy. *From the Founding of the City.* Trans. by B. O. Foster. London: Heinemann, 1922.

Lloyd, G.E.R. *Early Greek Science: Thales to Aristotle.* New York: Norton, 1970.

———. *Greek Science After Aristotle.* New York: Norton, 1973.

McLachlan, James. *American Boarding Schools: A Historical Study.* New York: Charles Scribner's Sons, 1970.

McLuhan, Marshall. *Understanding Media.* New York: McGraw-Hill, 1964.

Mao Tse-tung. *Four Essays on Philosophy.* Peking: Foreign Languages, 1968.

Marrou, H.I. *A History of Education in Antiquity.* New York: New American Library, 1964.

Mason, Charlotte M. *An Essay Towards a Philosophy of Education: A Liberal Education for All.* London: Dent, 1931.

Mazzini, Joseph. *The Duties of Man.* London: Dent, 1966.

Merton, Thomas. *The Seven Storey Mountain.* Garden City, N.Y.: Image Books, 1970.

Mill, John Stuart. *Autobiography.* New York: Columbia University, 1944.

Montaigne. *The Essays of Montaigne.* New York: Random House, 1933.

Mueller, Gustav Emil. *Plato: The Founder of Philosophy as Dialectic.* New York: Philosophical Library, 1965.

New English Bible. New York: Oxford University, 1976.

Newman, John Henry. "The Idea of a University." In *Thackeray, Newman, et al.,* edited by Charles W. Eliot, pp. 31-61. New York: P.F. Collier & Son, 1969.

Origio, Iris. "The Education of Renaissance Man." *Horizon* 2 (January 1960): 57-73.

Ortega y Gasset, José. *Phenomenology and Art.* New York: Norton, 1975.

———. *The Revolt of the Masses.* New York: Norton, 1932.

Pater, Walter. *The Renaissance*. New York: Random House.

Polybius. *The Histories*. London: Heinemann, 1960.

Ruskin, John. *Unto This Last*. London: Dent, 1968.

Russell, Bertrand. *On Education*. London: Unwin Books, 1973.

Sayers, Dorothy. *The Song of Roland*. Harmondsworth: Penguin Books, 1973.

Schumacher, E.F. *A Guide for the Perplexed*. New York: Harper & Row, 1977.

Sizer, Theodore. *Places for Learning, Places for Joy: Speculations on American School Reform*. Cambridge, Mass.: Harvard University Press, 1973.

Thucydides. *The History of the Peloponnesian War*. Oxford: Oxford University, 1973.

Tocqueville, Alexis de. *Democracy in America*. Edited by Richard D. Heffner. New York: New American Library, 1956.

Toynbee, Arnold. *A Study of History*. London: Oxford University, 1962.

Trypanis, Constantine A. *The Penguin Book of Greek Verse*. Harmondsworth: Penguin, 1971.

Vlastos, Gregory. "What Is Required of Us?" *University: A Princeton Quarterly* 65 (Summer 1975):2-5.

Weaver, Richard. *Visions of Order*. Baton Rouge: Louisiana State University, 1964.

Whitehead, A.N. *Science and the Modern World*. New York: Macmillan, 1929.

Wilson, Edmund. *To the Finland Station*. London: Macmillan, 1972.

Wouk, Herman. *The Caine Mutiny*. Garden City, N.Y.: Doubleday, 1951.

INDEX

ABOUT THE AUTHOR

David V. Hicks is President of St. Andrew's School in Jackson, Mississippi. Before moving to Jackson he worked as a curriculum consultant at the Westminster Schools in Atlanta.

Mr. Hicks has served on the faculty of strategy and policy at the Naval War College in Newport, Rhode Island, where he also lived and taught at St. George's School. For two years he lectured on the humanities at Briarcliff College, New York, working concurrently in the college's administration.

Mr. Hicks holds an A.B. from Princeton University and an M.A. from Oxford University, which he attended as a Rhodes scholar.